The Irreversible Crisis

D1602772

Also by Harry Magdoff and Paul M. Sweezy:

The Dynamics of U.S. Capitalism:
Corporate Structure, Inflation, Credit, Gold, and the Dollar (1972)

The End of Prosperity:
The American Economy in the 1970s (1977)

The Deepening Crisis of U.S. Capitalism (1981)

Stagnation and the Financial Explosion (1987)

The Irreversible Crisis

Crisis

five essays
by Harry Magdoff
and Paul M. Sweezy

Monthly Review Press
New York

Library of Congress Cataloging-in-Publication Data

The Irreversible crisis: five essays / [edited] by Harry
  Magdoff and Paul M. Sweezy.
      p.   cm.
    ISBN 0-85345-776-X:
    1. Business cycles. 2. Economic forecasting.
    3. Capitalism.
    4. Marxian economics. I. Magdoff, Harry. II. Sweezy,
    P. M. (Paul Marlor), 1910–   .
    HB3711.I77   1988   88–38856
    338.5′42′0973—dc19   CIP

Monthly Review Press
122 West 27th Street
New York, N.Y. 10001

Manufactured in the United States of America

10 9 8 7 6 5 4 3 2 1

Contents

Stagnation and the Financial Explosion

In the "Afterword to the Second German Edition" of *Das Kapital* Marx called attention to an aspect of the history of economic thought in the nineteenth century which, though in an entirely different context, has had a striking analogue in our time. The period from 1820 to 1830, he wrote, was notable in

England for scientific activity in the domain of political economy. It was the time as well of the vulgarizing and extending of Ricardo's theory, as of the contest of that theory with the old school. Splendid tournaments were held. . . . The unprejudiced character of this polemic—although the theory of Ricardo already serves, in exceptional cases, as a weapon of attack on bourgeois economy—is explained by the circumstances of the time. . . . The literature of political economy in England at this time calls to mind the stormy forward movement in France after Dr. Quesnay's death, but only as a St. Martin's summer reminds us of spring. With the year 1830 came the decisive change.

In France and in England the bourgeoisie had conquered political power. Thenceforth the class struggle, practically as well as theoretically, took on more and more outspoken forms. It sounded the knell of bourgeois economy. . . . It was thenceforth no longer a question whether this theorem or that was true, but whether it was useful to capital or harmful, expedient or inexpedient, politically dangerous or not. In place of disinterested inquirers there were hired prizefighters; in place of genuine scientific research, the bad conscience and the evil intent of apologetic.

Marx wrote this in 1872 at the dawn of the modern imperialist era and shortly after the defeat of the Paris Com-

7

mune. The class struggle in the advanced capitalist countries entered a new phase, and so did bourgeois economics with the triumph of the marginal utility schools in Austria, France, and Britain in the early 1870s. There followed roughly a half century of relative social peace and complacent economic theorizing, climaxed by the "New Era" of Henry Ford and "endless prosperity."

Then came the Crash of 1929, the Great Depression, and the deepening stagnation of the 1930s. Social struggles, in both the international and class arenas, intensified. Mainstream economics was stunned and helpless. The threatened bourgeoisies of the advanced capitalist countries reacted in two ways, exemplified by Nazi Germany and New Deal America.

Under these circumstances, the need for a new theory to help account for what was happening and to show the way to remedial policies was obvious and urgent. John Maynard Keynes met the challenge. As the most prestigious member of the Cambridge school, he was in a position to be listened to; as a brilliant theorist with a deep instinct for the survival of both England and capitalism, he appreciated the gravity of the situation and the necessity to escape from the confines of traditional economic dogmas. The publication in 1936 of his *General Theory of Employment, Interest and Money* signalled a revolution in economic thought comparable to that wrought by Adam Smith and David Ricardo a century and a half earlier.

But no revolution is without its counter-revolution. The stalwarts of the economics profession, regrouping their battered forces, moved to expunge the Keynesian heresy; and what looked like developing into a "splendid tournament," reminiscent of those of the period 1820–30, soon began to fill the pages not only of the professional economic journals but also of the business press and even the popular media. The form of this polemic was determined by the events of 1937–38. A recovery from the Great Depression that followed the crash of 1929 began in 1933 and continued, slowly but without serious interruption, for the next four years. Unemployment declined from 25 to 15 percent of the labor force, and things seemed on the way back to normal. Then, in the summer of 1937, the sky fell in. A sharp recession pushed unemployment back up to 19 percent in a few months, with no sign of resumed progress to be seen. Suddenly not only the economic profession but the country as a whole was faced with the question that could no longer be ignored or evaded: *Full Recovery or Stagnation?** The government itself soon joined the fray with the appointment by President Roosevelt of a Temporary National Economic Committee (TNEC), perhaps the most elaborate official inquiry into the condition of the economy ever mounted in this or any other country. Well-publicized hearings with star witnesses were held, and literally dozens of monographic studies were commissioned.

But the whole enterprise was short-lived. Even before the TNEC could issue its anticlimactic report, attention shifted dramatically from the sputtering economy to the Second World War. War orders came pouring in from Britain and France, and the United States began its own build-up for entry into the conflict two years later. The concerns of the 1930s were put aside as the U.S. economy spurted forward: by 1944 the GNP had increased by more than three quarters, and unemployment had sunk to less than 2 percent of the labor force.

Memories of stagnation lingered on, however, and this became a significant force in restraining the exuberance of the aftermath boom that normally follows a destructive war. It was not until the 1950s that the business community was converted to a mood of long-run optimism that was to contribute in its turn to the prolongation of the upswing that characterized the early postwar decades. The economics profession was quicker to forget the past. The interrupted debate of the 1930s was never revived; and even the publication in 1952 of the most thorough and penetrating study ever made on the problem of stagnation—Josef Steindl's *Maturity and Stagnation in American Capitalism*—was hardly noticed in the scholarly journals here or abroad.

---

*This is the title of a collection of essays published in 1938 by Professor Alvin Hansen of Harvard, the most prominent of Keynes's followers on this side of the Atlantic and, along with Professor Joseph Schumpeter, also of Harvard, a leading protagonist in the developing polemic of the late 1930s.

The virtual disappearance of practical and scientific interest in the extraordinary—and at the time totally unanticipated—events of the 1930s did not, however, signify any change in the underlying forces at work. In its innermost essence capitalism has always been a process of capital accumulation, and at no time in its history has this process been smooth or uninterrupted. This unevenness has been most evident and violent in the "normal" business cycle, universally recognized by all schools of economic thought. But it has manifested itself as well in longer waves of speeded-up and retarded growth. Until the 1930s, the interest of economists was mostly focused on the business cycle, with the longer waves only rarely being subjected to serious economic analysis. But what happened during that decade forced a recognition, at least for a brief time, that the cycle operates within the context of the longer waves, and that the latter also need to be analyzed and understood. Unfortunately, as related above, the effort to satisfy this need was cut short, and the economics profession generally reverted to its earlier stance of blocking out all but the short-term phenomena of the "normal" cycle.

This was, to put it mildly, the path of least resistance: no one who counted for anything—in business, in government, in academia—wanted to be reminded of the 1930s; and anyone who, like the present writers, kept insisting that, given the nature of the capitalist system, what had happened in the past not only could but almost certainly would happen again, was dismissed as hopelessly out of date and obviously incapable of understanding the "new economics" as preached by the high priests of the new capitalist faith.

It is true that for a while in the 1970s stagnation in the guise of "stagflation" crept back into the economists' (and the public's) consciousness. But there was little inclination to take it seriously, and nothing faintly resembling the deeply concerned debates of the late 1930s emerged. And when Ronald Reagan came along with his unique brand of "Voodoo" economics—the motto and guiding principle of which should be "après moi le deluge"—the ideologues of the ruling class, many of whom certainly knew better, distinguished themselves by hailing the great recovery of the 1980s and professing to believe that it marks but the beginning of a new golden era of economic expansion.

Now, in the winter of 1988, reality is well on the way to putting an end to this demeaning farce. The recovery that began at the end of 1982 has palpably run its course. As in the summer of 1937, when the upswing dating from 1933 suddenly collapsed, no restarting of the engine of capital accumulation is in prospect. The stimulatory medicine that Keynesian theory prescribes for depressions—massive doses of deficit spending—has already been used up. There is nothing left in the entire bag of tricks. The reality of stagnation on a scale not experienced for half a century now stares us in the face. It is high time for the Great Debate to be resumed.

We offer this book—the fifth in a series dating back to 1972—as a contribution to this crucially important enterprise.* Like its predecessors, it brings together essays originally published in *Monthly Review* that seek to analyze the current condition and direction of movement of the U.S. and global capitalist economies. Stagnation has of course been a recurrent—one might say ever-present—topic in these essays, and the purpose of this introduction so far has been to put this theme into meaningful, if all too sketchy, historical perspective. But long experience has taught us that there are other questions that need to be touched on in an introduction to a collection of this kind.

We both reached adulthood during the 1930s, and it was then that we received our initiation into the realities of capitalist economics and politics. For us economic stagnation in its most agonizing and pervasive form, including its far-reaching ramifications in every aspect of social life, was an overwhelming personal experience. We know what it is and what it can mean; we do not need elaborate definitions or explanations.

---

*The earlier ones are *The Dynamics of U.S. Capitalism: Corporate Structure, Inflation, Credit, Gold, and the Dollar* (1972); *The End of Prosperity: The American Economy in the 1970s* (1977); *The Deepening Crisis of U.S. Capitalism* (1981); and *Stagnation and the Financial Explosion* (1987).

But we have gradually learned, not altogether to our surprise of course, that younger people who grew up in the 1940s or later not only do not share but also do not understand these perceptions. The economic environment of the war and postwar periods that played such an important part in shaping their experiences was very different. For them, stagnation tends to be a rather vague term, equivalent perhaps to a longer-than-usual recession but with no implication of possible grave political and international repercussions. Under these circumstances, they find it hard to relate to what they are likely to regard as our obsession with the problem of stagnation. They are not quite sure what we are talking about or what all the fuss is over.

There is a temptation to say: just wait and see, you'll find out soon enough. Indeed, this may be the only really satisfactory answer. Unless backed up by actual experience, explanations often mean little. And there is no doubt that what we see as indications of stagnation in the 1970s and 1980s are still a long way from the realities of half a century ago. But it would be a cop-out to leave it at that. We owe it to our readers at least to try to make clearer what we mean by stagnation and why we think it is so important.

It may be useful to begin with a quotation from an article in a recent issue of the *Journal of Post Keynesian Economics*. In the half century ending in 1983, according to the authors,

there have been only ten years (ignoring World War II and conversion) in which actual GNP has equaled or exceeded potential. Those ten years have been noteworthy for the presence of expansionary government. Unfortunately, most of the expansion was war-laden. Three of those years (1950–52) were during the Korean War; five of them were during the Vietnam War, which overlapped the activist, Kennedy-Johnson, Keynesian, civilian expansionist regimes. Without the strong pull from government demand over the last half century, the civilian economy has achieved its potential only in 1956 and 1973. Even those two years, on the basis of the utilization of human resources (unemployment) criterion, were significantly inferior to 1929.*

Though hardly comparable to the gloomy performance of the 1930s, this record does clearly indicate that the forces that were then overwhelmingly dominant had by no means disappeared in the new postwar climate. What did change—and this is a matter of crucial importance that economic theory has only begun to recognize and deal with—is the way the economy as a whole has adjusted to and been reshaped by the persistent tendency of society's utilization of productive resources to lag behind its huge and growing potential. Whereas in the earlier period this tendency worked itself out in a catastrophic collapse of production—during the 1930s as a whole, unemployment and utilization of productive capacity averaged 18 percent and 63 percent respectively—in the postwar period economic energies, instead of lying dormant, have increasingly been channelled into a variety of wasteful, parasitic, and generally unproductive uses. This has been an enormously complex process that is still very imperfectly understood (in fact, mainstream economics does not even recognize its existence); the point to be emphasized here is that far from having eliminated the stagnationist tendencies inherent in today's mature monopoly capitalist economy, this process has forced these tendencies to take on new forms and disguises. At the same time, it is necessary to emphasize that these changes in the *form* of stagnation do not mean that the possibility of a generalized collapse of the whole structure no longer exists. This is a "problematic" that has come increasingly to the fore in the last few years, and it is one that is very much in our minds as we write this introduction.

Among the forces counteracting the tendency to stagnation, none has been more important or less understood by economic analysts than the growth, beginning in the 1960s and rapidly gaining momentum after the severe recession of the

---

*John F. Walker and Harold G. Vattner, "Stagnation—Performance and Policy: A Comparison of the Depression Decade with 1973–1984," *Journal of Post Keynesian Economics,* Summer 1986, p. 525.

mid-1970s, of the country's debt structure (government, corporate, and individual) at a pace far exceeding the sluggish expansion of the underlying "real" economy. The result has been the emergence of an unprecedentedly huge and fragile financial superstructure subject to stresses and strains that increasingly threaten the stability of the economy as a whole. This should become clearer as we present updated evidence on these developments.

The dramatic change in the role of debt is clearly revealed in Chart 1, which compares the total outstanding public and private debt with Gross National Product (GNP). Debt is of course a natural and necessary ingredient of a business economy. In the normal course of events, it grows in tandem with business activity, slowing down or declining during business downturns and expanding to fuel recoveries. And that was the way it went prior to the renewed onset of stagnation. Thus, the ratio of outstanding debt to GNP hovered around 1.5 between 1950 and 1960. But a change in the relationship had already begun to show up during the 1960s: debt started to accumulate at a somewhat faster rate than GNP. This can be seen in the widening of the gap between the two lines. A spectacular shift, however, became manifest in the 1970s: the more stagnation spread, the greater the reliance on debt as a prop to the economy. As can be seen from the chart, the gap between the two lines accelerated after 1970. Between 1970 and 1980, the ratio of debt to GNP advanced from 1.57 to 1.7. That, it turned out, was only a prelude to the debt explosion in the 1980s. By 1987, the total outstanding debt was 2.25 times as large as that year's GNP.

Especially significant is the way the increasing reliance on debt permeated every area of the economy. This can be seen in the growth patterns of debt in each of the four major components of the economy, presented in Table 1. The first line of the table includes state and local as well as federal indebtedness. In view of all the attention paid by the media and analysts to this area, it is useful to note that the rise in government borrowing was less than that of any of the other categories. In fact, government debt as a percentage of the total declined from 34

Chart 1
Outstanding Debt and Gross National Product

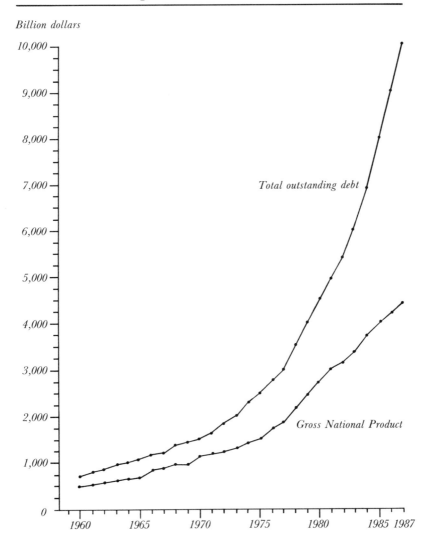

Billion dollars

10,000 —

9,000 —

8,000 —

7,000 —

6,000 —

5,000 —

4,000 —

3,000 —

2,000 —

1,000 —

0 —

Total outstanding debt

Gross National Product

1960   1965   1970   1975   1980   1985 1987

Source: Federal Reserve Board, *Flow of Funds Accounts* and *Survey of Current Business*, February, 1986.

Table 1
Outstanding Debt
(*Index numbers: 1965 = 100*)

Borrower	1965	1970	1975	1980	1987
Government[a]	100	123.1	182.4	284.0	688.0
Consumers[b]	100	139.9	222.1	422.5	840.0
Nonfinancial business	100	165.8	277.7	474.2	969.2
Financial business	100	199.7	432.2	933.7	2972.4
Total	100	144.8	236.1	418.6	944.7

Notes: a) Includes federal, state, and local governments.
b) This category is called "households" in the source of these statistics. Although consumers are the overwhelming component, the data also include personal trusts, nonprofit foundations, private schools and hospitals, labor unions, and churches.

Source: Federal Reserve Board, *Flow of Funds Accounts.*

percent in 1965 to 25 percent in 1987. What is particularly noteworthy, however, is that here as elsewhere debt dependency in the last fifteen years has been steadily increasing to compensate for a weakening private economy. Total government expenditures have been a major economic influence throughout the post-Second World War years, rising from 13.5 percent of GNP in 1950 to 20.4 percent in 1987. But while in the earlier years, surpluses in good years more or less balanced the deficits of recession periods, later on the pattern changed. Deficits began gradually to outweigh surpluses during the 1960s, and thereafter reliance on deficits rapidly increased. During the 1970s as a whole, deficits were needed to pay for 8 percent of federal government expenditures, whereas during the first seven years of the present decade this proportion more than doubled to 17 percent.

The rise in consumer debt shown in the second line of the table has been fostered by two factors: a strong desire to own homes and cars on the one hand, and an energetic promotion of lending by banks and finance companies on the other. Whenever the effective demand for these big-ticket items showed a tendency to taper off, lending terms were eased to widen the market. This practice was stimulated not only by manufacturers and house builders, but also by finance companies seeking a bigger share of this profitable business. But while this activity has propped up sales of homes and consumer durable goods, it has also piled up a mountain of consumer debt that is fast approaching an unsustainable limit: in 1970 the outstanding consumer debt amounted to about 67 percent of after-tax consumer income; in 1987 it was close to 90 percent.

As can be seen from line 3 of the table, nonfinancial business has been no stranger to the feverish accumulation of debt. The dominant component of this category of course consists of corporations, some of which have undertaken major debt obligations to keep alive, and are hence forced to keep on borrowing just to meet payments on past debt. Others, in contrast, have long been awash with idle cash, and many of these have also joined the parade. Unable to find profitable productive investment opportunities in the face of excess capacity and flagging demand, they have been eager participants in the merger, takeover, and leveraged buyout frenzy that has swept the country in recent years, becoming in the process both lenders and borrowers on an enormous scale. For all these reasons, nonfinancial corporations as a whole now carry a debt load of about $1.5 trillion, which, according to Felix Rohatyn, of the Lazard Frères investment banking firm, exceeds their total net worth by 12 percent. Moreover, Rohatyn points out, since 1982 the cost of servicing this debt has been absorbing 50 percent of the entire corporate cash flow. By comparison, during the 1976–79 recovery this cost averaged only 27 percent.*

But the most startling rate of growth in borrowing occurred in the financial sector itself (line 4 of Table 1). To a certain extent the numbers give an exaggerated impression of what actually happened. Since the debt of financial firms was relatively small in the base year, the rate of increase shows up as

---

*Felix G. Rohatyn in an address given before the Joint Economic Committee 40th Anniversary Symposium, Washington, D.C., January 16, 1986.

abnormally large when compared with the sectors that already had a much more substantial debt at the outset. Yet the transformation of the firms that are at the core of the debt explosion from minor to major borrowers is itself significant. Traditionally, most of these enterprises are intermediaries that receive otherwise idle funds, which are then lent out. But in the new financial environment, these firms have gone far beyond the role of intermediaries. They have themselves become large borrowers, thus stimulating a more rapid and intensive circulation of the economy's cash reserves.

Once started, this self-expansion of the financial sector has turned into a complex and enormously powerful process with the most far-reaching consequences. The following summary of what has happened and the resulting changes in the financial picture is especially interesting in that it comes, as one might say, from the horse's mouth—the Federal Reserve Bank of New York:

> The volatility of prices for the entire spectrum of financial assets has risen considerably. In step with this development, new financial instruments—such as futures, options, and swaps—that provide additional ways to transfer price risks among market participants flourished. The active trading of these new instruments and of the more conventional instruments underlying them has burgeoned. The volume of financial transactions has accelerated at an unprecedented rate.
>
> Competition has greatly increased in the whole range of financial services. Commercial banks, thrift institutions, investment banks, and insurance companies are all expanding the range of their activities and crossing over into each other's traditional business preserves. Nonfinancial businesses are directly entering financial services as well. And foreign financial institutions are increasing their involvement in markets here at the same time that U.S. firms are expanding abroad. Competitive pressures have been compounded by the ongoing trend toward financial deregulation of the terms that institutions can charge or offer, the kinds of transactions in which they may engage, and the geographical markets they may enter. This increased degree of competition has squeezed earnings margins on many conventional financial activities, accelerating the development and diffusion of innovations.

The weakened economic and financial condition of major sectors—energy, agriculture, commercial real estate, and various developing countries—has diminished the credit standing of many borrowers. One consequence has been that in recent years the costs of capital and funding for some bank lenders to those sectors have tended to rise relative to the costs for high quality commercial credits. At the same time, the direct credit markets have become more accessible to business borrowers. Banks have had a difficult time competing with the commercial paper and securities markets for corporate credit demands, especially those of the "blue chip" firms. Indeed, in many cases, banks have sought to profit from the trend toward market financing by generating loans and selling them off, either directly or packaged as securities, or by expanding their roles as guarantors and distributors of capital market instruments.

All these forces—innovation, competition, deregulation, securitization, and the growth of trading—have combined to create a challenging environment.*

The fact that the essay from which this passage comes constitutes the bulk of a recent annual report of the New York Federal Reserve Bank is of special significance. In the past these annual reports have been rather humdrum summaries of business and banking developments in the preceding year. The decision to depart from tradition was made, according to the Bank's president, because "the rapid transformations in the markets are unprecedented in their scope." In fact, there can be little doubt that the real reason was not to supply information but rather to press the alarm button. The essay starts off by noting that "extraordinary economic imbalances and financial strains have marked the course of the recovery." Although most of the danger spots are only gently hinted at, one specific reference to a potential disaster area boggles the mind:

And last November a major clearing bank for securities transactions experienced a severe computer problem that could not be put right before closing. As a consequence, this Bank extended a record $22.6 billion loan on an overnight basis.

That incident was well-contained and did not threaten to spill

---

*Edward J. Frydl, vice-president and assistant director of research, "The Challenge of Financial Change," Federal Bank of New York, *Annual Report*, 1985.

over to other institutions or markets. The computer difficulties were resolved the next day. But it dramatically points out the types of risks we face. Settlement disrupts stemming from more protracted operational problems may not be so limited in their consequences. And, of course, a settlement failure stemming from a default could play havoc throughout the financial system.

The possibility of settlement failures is only one of the areas of financial fragility, all of which, as the above quote implies, are parts of an extensive worldwide network of financial operations. Consciousness of this is what lies behind the warning, issued more recently by William Seidman, chairman of the Federal Deposit Insurance Corporation:

> The financial area is probably, next to nuclear war, the kind of area that can get out of control, and once out of control cannot be contained and will probably do more to upset the civilized world than about anything you can think of.*

Aware as the monetary authorities may be of the dangers that lie ahead, their hands are nonetheless tied. And the reason is precisely the fragility of the system. Interference by the government or the monetary authorities, other than efforts to put out fires when they flare up, carries with it the potential of setting off a chain reaction. This explains why at every critical juncture existing restraints on further financial expansion have been relaxed in order to avoid a major breakdown. The removal of controls has in turn opened the door to still more innovations that add to the fragility.

What is especially striking in the present situation is that the more the financial system has moved away from its role as facilitator of the production and distribution of goods and services, the more it has taken on a life of its own, a fact that can be seen most vividly in the mushrooming of speculative activity, which is closely tied in with the debt explosion of the last ten years, as well as with the day-to-day-operations of financial firms. Felix Rohatyn, an acute observer of the financial scene, claimed in the talk cited above that today we have the "most

---

*Cited in the *Financial Times*, May 29, 1986. It should come as no surprise that a banker equates the "civilized world" with capitalism.

unfettered speculation seen in this country since 1929." One indication of this is the jump in the average number of shares of stock traded *daily* on the New York Stock Exchange, from 19 million in 1975 to over 200 million in 1987. Even more striking is the way the futures markets have come to dominate gambling activities. Back in 1960, futures contracts related almost entirely to commodities: in that year only 3.9 million contracts were written. This activity grew to 11.2 million in 1970, which was still within reason, given the growth in the economy. But the 1970s were a different story: by the middle of that decade, futures markets had been established in precious metals, foreign currency, and financial instruments. Other innovations followed (betting on the future of average stock prices, for example), and the dam burst. In 1980 over 92 million futures contracts were traded, in 1987 over 220 million, with still no end in sight. This has become a major "growth industry" in the United States and is fast spreading to other major capitalist centers abroad.

Chart 2, comparing an index of the volume of futures trading with the Federal Reserve Board's index of industrial production, presents a graphic picture of this speculative explosion. Prior to 1970, futures trading grew at roughly the same pace as production. But then the economic slowdown of the 1970s set in, and production lagged while speculation skyrocketed. Since 1977, industrial production has increased 30 percent, the volume of futures trading by over 400 percent! It is little wonder that *Business Week* (16 September 1985) editorialized: "Slow growth and today's rampant speculative binge are locked in some kind of symbiotic embrace."

Acknowledgment of this "symbiotic embrace," however, leaves open the question of which is cause and which effect. A popular line of thought places the blame on speculation (including the hectic buying and selling of corporations) as the cause of the country's industrial malaise. But for the diversion of funds to these wasteful activities, the argument holds, capital would be flowing into useful productive investment. On the other hand, Henry Kaufman, former managing director of the Salomon Brothers investment banking firm and one of Wall

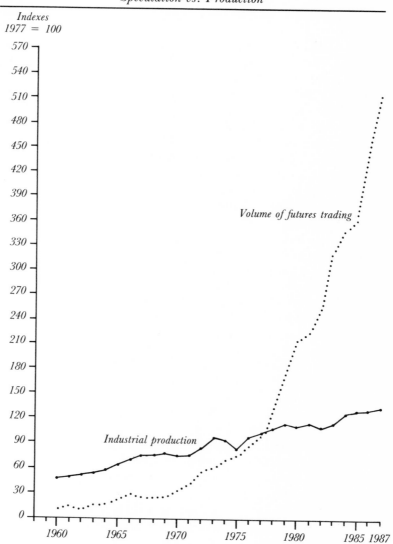

Chart 2
Speculation vs. Production

Indexes
1977 = 100

570 —

540 —

510 —

480 —

450 —

420 —

390 —

360 —   *Volume of futures trading*

330 —

300 —

270 —

240 —

210 —

180 —

150 —

120 —

90 —   *Industrial production*

60 —

30 —

0 —

1960   1965   1970   1975   1980   1985 1987

Source: Futures Trading Association and Federal Reserve Board.

Table 2
Growth of the Financial Sector

| | Gross National Product | | Financial sector |
| | Goods production^a | Financial firms^b | as a percent of |
	(Billions of dollars)		goods production
1950	153.3	32.2	21.0
1960	250.5	72.8	29.1
1970	440.7	145.8	33.1
1980	1144.6	400.6	35.0
1987	1660.6	775.4	46.7

Notes: a) Agriculture, mining, construction, manufacturing, transportation, and public utilities.
b) Banks, other finance companies, real estate, and insurance.

Source: National income and product accounts, as reported in *Survey of Current Business*, various issues.

Street's most astute analysts, sees it just the other way around: "The rapid expansion in bank reserves against a sluggish economic backdrop yielded the classic result: funds sought financial assets, given that there was no need to finance real economic activity."*

Kaufman's view is clearly the realistic one. It should be obvious that capitalists will not invest in additional capacity when their factories and mines are already able to produce more than the market can absorb. Excess capacity emerged in one industry after another long before the extraordinary surge of speculation and finance in the 1970s, and this was true not only in the United States but throughout the advanced capitalist world. The shift in emphasis from industrial to pecuniary pursuits is equally international in scope.

The growing relative importance of "making money," as distinct from "making goods," in the U.S. economy is highlighted in Table 2. The first column presents the dollar amounts of GNP accounted for by industries engaged in producing and

---

*Henry Kaufman, "In the Shadow of Financial Exhilaration," *Challenge*, July-August 1986.

shipping goods (agriculture, mining, construction, manufacturing, transportation, and public utilities) in selected years from 1950 to 1987. The second column gives the dollar amounts of GNP attributed to the financial sector (finance, real estate, and insurance) in the same years. As can be seen, in 1950 the financial sector's contribution to GNP was 21 percent that of the goods sector; by 1987 this had more than doubled to 46.7 percent. Without doubt this reflects a structural change of unprecedented magnitude.

At this point we would do well to pause and reflect on the larger meaning of the dramatic developments of recent years that have been briefly passed in review in the last few pages. Underlying our analysis here and throughout this volume is a theory which, stripped to its barest essentials, sees the mature monopoly capitalist economy as one that is subject to, and indeed dominated by, a basic contradiction: the very growth of its productive potential puts insuperable obstacles in the way of making full use of available human and material resources for the satisfaction of the needs of the great mass of the population. What this means is (1) that in the absence of sufficiently powerful counteracting forces, the normal state of the economy is stagnation; and (2) that the real history of the system in its monopoly capitalist phase is determined by the interaction of the tendency to stagnation and the forces acting counter to this tendency.

On the face of it, this dialectic appears to be quite symmetrical—force versus counterforce, now one and now the other having the upper hand and neither able to establish long-run domination. But this is an illusion. The tendency to stagnation is inherent in the system, deeply rooted and in continuous operation. The counter-tendencies, on the other hand, are varied, intermittent, and (most important) self-limiting. We can best appreciate this lack of symmetry, not by an abstract argument but by a quick review of the history of the last half century. Stagnation reigned supreme in the 1930s, the counteracting forces generated by the First World War and its aftermath having exhausted their strength by 1929. The Second

World War put an end to this phase; and the normal aftermath boom took over and played a dominant role for an unusually long period—during which, however, as noted above, the manifestations of the tendency to stagnation never completely disappeared. By the 1970s the forces that powered the long aftermath expansion finally petered out, and stagnation once again rose to dominance. At this juncture, a new set of counteracting forces which have been the focus of our analysis in this introduction went into operation, braking the slide into stagnation and maintaining for a few years a precarious balance between the underlying tendency and the counteracting forces. Once again, however, the latter have shown themselves to be essentially unstable and temporary. As we write these lines, the financial explosion that speeded up so dramatically in the Reagan period is more and more obviously headed for a crisis.

If this analysis is correct, it has extremely important implications for all those, whether they consider themselves to be on the left or not, who are dissatisfied with the way the economy has been functioning in recent years. The reason is that it rules out the possibility of successful remedial action that leaves intact the system's basic structure and working principles—or, in other words, that does not call into question the primacy of profit-making and capital-accumulation as the purpose and motor force of economic activity. Stagnation theory tells us—and history confirms—that a system so oriented and motivated is not, as mainstream economics has always claimed, a self-adjusting and self-steering organism that automatically adheres to the path of long-run development. On the contrary, it is always tending to bog down under the weight of its own contradictions, and the conditions that foster a new lease on life, like major wars and speculative manias, do enormous damage and soon lose their efficacy.

Stagnation theory, in short, teaches us that what we need is not the reform of monopoly capitalism but its replacement by a system that organizes economic activity not for the greater glory of capital but to meet the needs of people to lead decent, secure, and, to the extent possible, creative lives. Once this lesson has been well and truly learned, we can give up the absurd fantasy of making a rotten system work for us, and buckle down to the increasingly urgent tasks of directly fighting for what ought to be the birthright of every member of a society that has any claim to consider itself free and democratic—a job, a steady income, a home, health care, and security in old age. If our ruling class and the government it controls cannot meet these elementary human demands, they should be thrown out and make way for another system that can and will. It is of course bound to be a long and difficult struggle, but it is the only one that makes sense.

Capitalism and the Distribution of Income and Wealth

In the beginning, capitalism came into a world of traditional societies based on small-scale peasant and artisan production. Trading relations between regions and, locally, between town and country, together with their associated monetary and credit arrangements, were already well-developed. Surplus product, over and above what was necessary for society's reproduction, accrued mostly to landlords and merchants who lived on a scale far above that of the great mass of the people. Nobles and kings, with their retainers and armies, took their share, lavishing much of the social surplus on costly displays and military adventures. These societies, though generally not stagnant, tended to expand slowly in step with population growth, and experienced ups and downs in response to the rhythms and vagaries of the natural environment.

In this setting, enterprising small traders and producers discovered that it would be possible to increase productivity and hence their own incomes by bringing groups of workers together under unified managements. In the initial stages, these new workshops utilized existing technologies, with the increases in productivity coming from the kinds of simple division of labor so lovingly described by Adam Smith in his celebrated example of an eighteenth-century pin manufactory. But soon a basic change occurred. These budding entrepreneurs, aided and abetted by their ablest workers, moved from refining existing technologies to introducing new ones, with emphasis rapidly shifting from mechanical improvements to the invention and installation of machinery. This process began in textiles, sweeping through the various branches of the industry (spinning, weaving, fulling, dyeing, etc.) in a sort of chain reaction. From there it spread to other industries, producing the great variety of goods required for social reproduction and for the satisfaction of the needs of an increasingly differentiated population. The last stage in the development of full-fledged capitalism came with the takeover by the new form of capitalist enterprise of the production of machinery (and other kinds of means of production) which had remained the domain of highly skilled workmen right up to the middle of the nineteenth century. With this, the circle was closed, and capitalism became a self-contained system with its own internal logic and its unprecedentedly powerful dynamic.

But if capitalism as a mode of production was fully formed by the mid-nineteenth century, this in no way implies that it was the quantitatively dominant mode of production. Even in its British heartland, capitalism was still very much a minority affair, and this was much more so in the less-developed capitalisms of the European and North American continents. This is an enormously important fact of economic history, almost always underemphasized and often completely overlooked. The overlooking typically takes the form of treating the countries in which capitalism had gained a foothold as though they were already fully capitalist in their economic and social structures. Following this procedure unfortunately results in obscuring the ways in which capitalism interacted with its precapitalist environment in the course of developing from its minority status in the nineteenth century to its overwhelmingly majority status in the second half of the twentieth century.

The problem that concerns us in the present context can be formulated as follows: what is the modus operandi of a "small" capitalism surrounded by a "large" noncapitalist environment? Here there are two conceptually distinguishable processes at work which in practice merge into one. On the one hand, the capitalist system has a strong tendency to expand *internally* as the individual capitals compete with each other to lower costs and take over larger shares of markets already incorporated into the circuits of capital. This of course requires additional capital investment which is typically financed out of profits plus whatever precapitalist receivers of rent and interest choose to channel into these new ways of increasing their income and wealth. On the other hand, capitalists have an equally strong urge to expand *externally* by taking over markets hitherto supplied by small noncapitalist producers, with the latter being thrown out of work and forced to join the labor force available for capitalist exploitation. This drive for external expansion also requires additional capital investment which is financed from the same sources as internal expansion. While the internal and external modes of capital expansion are, as already noted, conceptually distinguishable, in practice they are homogeneous and together constitute the overall process of capital accumulation which has been the central preoccupation of economic analysts throughout the capitalist period.

In the early stage of capitalist development, the potential for expansion, both internal and external, was obviously vast. What Marx called Department I, production of the means of production, had to be built up virtually from scratch; incorporating the traditional sectors of the economy into the capitalist orbit absorbed large amounts of capital; and, last but far from least, the infrastructure of roads, canals, ports, and finally railroads required to sustain a growing capitalist economy, was enormously costly in terms of both capital and labor (during the second half of the nineteenth century in the United States, railroads alone were responsible for more investment than all manufacturing industries together). So great indeed was the plainly visible actual and potential demand for new investment, that capitalist economic textbooks of the late nineteenth and early twentieth century tended to treat it for all practical purposes as unlimited.

The other side of the coin of course was the supply of investment capital which the textbooks labeled "saving," thus tacitly assuming (1) that the only source of funds to finance investment projects is the savings of capitalists and others with more income than they need to support their accustomed life style, and (2) that all such savings are actually channeled into investment. If these assumptions are accepted as reasonable approximations to reality, probably true enough in the earlier phases of capitalist development, the result was an enormous simplification of the analysis of the capital accumulation process as a whole.

Since the demand for saving could be considered unlimited, it followed that the speed of capital accumulation and, by implication, the rate of growth of society's wealth and well-being, became a simple function of the rate of saving. And the rate of saving in turn appeared to depend on two factors: (1) the rate of profit (workers were thought of as living close to the subsistence level and hence being incapable of saving, while it was taken for granted that capitalists would save more the bigger their incomes); and (2) the extent to which other recipients of social surplus in the form of rent and interest could be persuaded to act more like capitalists and less like free-spending aristocrats.

Against this background it is easy to understand how it happened that from its earliest days capitalism engendered and enthusiastically promoted the idea that inequality of income is an unalloyed social good, the more the better. To be sure, the vast majority of the population was abysmally poor, but it was not difficult to demonstrate that if all the wealth of the rich were evenly distributed among the poor, the average gain would be negligible and all hope for a better future would be dashed. The only way to go was to accelerate as much as possible the rate of capital accumulation. Accumulation, in Marx's words, was "Moses and the prophets," and the way to foster it was maximum inequality in the distribution of income. This became in a very real sense the keystone in the arch of capitalist ideology, the centerpiece without which the whole structure would collapse. And despite all the changes in the meantime, it remains in place today, essentially unchanged and still bearing its crucially important ideological load.

So much for the history of an idea—an idea which is some 200 years old and, at least in the advanced capitalist countries, seems to have as strong a grip on the minds of economists and statesmen as at any time in the past. Like all such powerful ideas, this one had its roots in the reality of the time and place of its origin: capital accumulation as an objective and saving as a means to its realization were indeed essential to the transition from the relatively static society of our ancestors to the highly dynamic society of our own time. Whether or not this was a good thing is of course debatable; what is not debatable is that it happened and that the process is not reversible. The question that needs to be addressed today, therefore, is whether capital accumulation, saving, and inequality in the distribution of income play the same role in the dynamics of our society as they did in the past.

Our answer is an unqualified no. Both on the demand side and on the supply side, the situation today is radically different from what it was when capitalism was in the process of establishing itself as the overwhelmingly dominant world system. Let us look at these two aspects of the problem in turn.

The Demand for Investment Capital

First, while the expansion of capitalism into its external environment has by no means ceased (witness the rapid penetration of capitalist relations into the service-producing areas of the economy), still there can be little doubt that this process is both relatively less important than it was in earlier times and bound to recede still further as the noncapitalist environment shrinks in size.

Second, the demand for investment capital to build up Department I, a factor that bulked large in the later nineteenth and early twentieth centuries, is of relatively minor importance today in the advanced capitalist countries. They all have highly developed capital-goods industries which, even in prosperous times, normally operate with a comfortable margin of excess capacity. The upkeep and modernization of these industries—and also of course of existing industries in Department II (consumer goods)—is provided for by depreciation reserves and generates no new net demand for investment capital.

Third, in the competitive stage of capitalism (roughly up to 1900) innovation and technological progress normally took the form of new firms with lower costs entering existing industries. As a result, higher-cost older firms were driven out of business, with their capital assets being drastically devalued or

even entirely wiped out. This process, which was responsible
for an important part of the demand for new capital investment, was superseded in the stage of monopoly capitalism.
Monopolistic (or oligopolistic) firms are generally in control of
their markets and able to regulate the rate of introduction of
new technology to preserve their profit margins. Assets that
would have been wiped out under competition are retained and
serve as a protective barrier against new competitors. What
Schumpeter called the competitive process of "creative de-
struction" is slowed down, and so also is the overall rate of new
investment.

Fourth is the role of new industries in the investment
process. If we go back far enough in the history of capitalism,
we come to a time when all industries were, from the capitalist
point of view, new industries and when the capitalist investment process encompassed both expansion into existing
noncapitalist areas and the creation of novel industries through
technological and product innovation. But as capitalism expands over time, the relative importance of new industries
recedes. They come to occupy a position on the margins of the
system rather than playing a key role in its central mechanism.
Only think, for example, of the impact of the railroad and the
automobile in the second half of the nineteenth century and
first half of the twentieth, respectively, compared to that of the
electronics-related industries of our time. The former directly
and indirectly dominated the demand for investment capital
for more than a century; while the latter, though enormously
dynamic in terms of technological and product innovation,
have never played a major, let alone a decisive, role in the
market for investment capital.

In summary, then, we can say that the demand for
investment capital, while virtually unlimited in the formative
days of the system, steadily declined to relatively minor dimensions as the system expanded and matured. It is even true that a
developed capitalist system such as that of the United States
today has the capacity to meet the needs of reproduction and
consumption with little or no net investment.

Not of course that such a situation is at all likely in

practice. But to understand this, we must turn from the demand side to the supply side of the capital investment equation.

The Supply of Investment Capital

In the beginning, while the demand for investment capital seemed virtually unlimited, the supply was narrowly restricted. Circumstances were favorable for a rapid increase in productivity, but under the pressure of intense competition average profit rates were kept down and much of the increase in output went into raising the very low level of wages inherited from the precapitalist era. In addition, the landlord and merchant classes, recipients of a large share of society's surplus product, were still imbued with precapitalist habits and only gradually came under the sway of the bourgeois moral imperative to consume less in the present in order to have more in the future.

Later on, as the transition from competitive to monopoly capitalism proceeded, the situation changed. Large corporations replaced small individual entrepreneurs as the dominant form of business enterprise. Competition took new forms that put less pressure on prices and profit rates. Capitalists bought land, and landlords became capitalists through investment in corporate securities. Banking developed from a largely modest helper of trade into a huge financial apparatus with greatly expanded functions and correspondingly increased power. As society's economic surplus grew, it increasingly gravitated into the hands of capitalists where it was more efficiently mobilized and made available for investment in profitable investment opportunities.

The Growing Imbalance of Demand and Supply

Our analysis to this point indicates that as capitalism develops from its early beginnings to its full-fledged maturity, there takes place a relative weakening of the demand for additional investment capital and a relative strengthening of the supply. These two contradictory tendencies can obviously coexist as long as demand exceeds supply: the consequence is simply a fast rate of growth, precisely the state of affairs always considered ideal by bourgeois ideologists. But if these tendencies continue to operate beyond the point of equilibrium—the point where the demand for investment capital begins to fall short of the supply—it would seem that trouble is bound to follow.

This was a problem that deeply concerned some of the classical economists—most notably Malthus and Sismondi—who tended to interpret the depressed economic conditions that followed the Napoleonic Wars as an indication of systemic failure. The fierce drive of capitalists to accumulate, so much admired by most of their fellow political economists, seemed to them to contain the danger of building up a productive apparatus too large for the combined needs of a working class condemned to live on subsistence wages and a resolutely abstemious capitalist class. By the middle years of the nineteenth century, particularly with the expansion of capital abroad, this worry largely subsided, though one can still detect traces of it in the writings of John Stuart Mill. It never altogether disappeared, however; and along with the prolonged depression of the 1870s, similar ideas of overproduction and/or underconsumption emerged, especially in the trade-union and socialist movements that began to come into their own in the closing decades of the nineteenth century.

It was just at this time too, and not accidentally, that bourgeois economic theory underwent its metamorphosis from classical political economy to neoclassical economics. Not surprisingly, one of the primary tasks of this new "science" was to demonstrate that there could be no such thing as overproduction or underconsumption, that the system had its own method of regulating the accumulation of capital in an optimum way.

Neoclassical theory sought to solve this problem by the device of treating investment capital exactly like any one of the other many commodities that together constitute the social product—bread, for example. If the demand for bread selling at 50¢ a loaf exceeds the supply, the price will rise and more bread will be produced; conversely if the supply exceeds the demand, the price will fall and less bread will be produced.

Demand, supply, and price are thus seen as mutually dependent variables that adjust to each other until an equilibrium position is reached in which demand equals supply at a price that covers the current cost of production.

At first glance it might seem impossible to apply this kind of market logic to the case of investment capital. There is no identifiable physical commodity with any such name, hence no quoted price, no particular quantities demanded or supplied, no cost of production. Capital (any kind of capital) starts off as a quantity of money but actually functions as capital only by being used to buy a heterogeneous collection of means of production. Capital as money has a kind of price (a rate of interest)—or rather a range of prices depending on a variety of surrounding conditions—but no identifiable or measurable cost of production. All in all, the notion that capital is like bread and subject to the normal logic of demand and supply seems hopelessly unrealistic.

Still, the economists were not deterred. It would take us too far afield to attempt to describe the heroic abstractions and drastic simplifications by means of which they forced this most complicated of economic problems into the straitjacket of received demand-and-supply analysis. Suffice it to say that this is one of the most tangled tales in the history of economic analysis, one that is still involved in learned and sometimes heated discussions. For present purposes we only need the most simplified sketch of what had become standard textbook doctrine by the time of the Great Depression of the 1930s.

Capital was conceptualized as a physical quantity of an imaginary, all-purpose, flexible and divisible, "produced means of production" entering into the production process as a "factor of production" in exactly the same way as land and labor, the other two traditional factors of production. Just as "rent" and "wages" are the prices of land and labor, so "interest" is the price of capital. In all three cases, the price reflects the "marginal productivity" of the respective factors and provides a corresponding income to their owners, i.e., the landlords, the workers, and the capitalists. Production is organized by "entrepreneurs" who employ and combine the factors of production and receive a "normal" rate of profit (sometimes also called a "wage of management") for their distinctive services.

If in such a system all prices are in equilibrium and owners of the factors of production spend their entire income on consumer goods, the system would simply reproduce itself from one year to the next. In other words it would be what classical political economy had called a stationary state. But of course in the real world capitalism never behaved this way: from the beginning its main features have been growth and change, with the accumulation of capital providing the prime motive power. The problem therefore was to integrate this essentially dynamic process into the demand-and-supply framework.

Entrepreneurs were posited as the demanders of capital, and capitalists as the suppliers. The equilibrator of the two (as in the case of bread) was the price, i.e., the rate of interest. The key to the whole analysis was therefore a presumed set of relations between the demand for capital, the rate of interest, and the supply. If, as our earlier analysis indicated, the development of capitalism tends to produce a relative decline in the demand and a relative increase in the supply, the result should be a more or less continuous fall in the rate of interest. This in turn is assumed to stimulate demand (because entrepreneurs can profitably undertake projects that were previously too costly) and reduce supply (because capitalists get less income from their investments and are hence assumed to consume more and save less). The conclusion of course was that there could never be any lasting disequilibrium between the demand and supply of investment capital.

This was perhaps the crowning achievement of neoclassical economics. A "scientific" solution was provided for what had long been a troublesome problem. Everything was really for the best in the best of all possible worlds.

The only trouble was that the resemblance between the theory and reality grew more and more tenuous as capitalism matured into its twentieth-century monopolistic form. The breaking point finally came with the Great Depression. The accumulation process came to an abrupt halt after the 1929 crash, and by the mid-1930s it showed only the feeblest signs of recovery. The stage was set for a revolt from within the ranks of the economists themselves.

The revolt, appropriately enough, was led by John Maynard Keynes, the leading light in the Cambridge school, itself the main inheritor of the tradition of British economic thought stretching back to Adam Smith and David Ricardo. The focus of the revolt was precisely the supposed self-regulating character of the accumulation process. The gist of Keynes's argument was that under conditions of advanced capitalism investors and savers are two quite separate groups each motivated by its own particular concerns and interests. The smooth functioning of the economy depends on their actions being coordinated in such a way that what the investors want to invest equals what the savers want to save. But there is no mechanism to bring this about;* and if entrepreneurs actually want to invest less than savers want to save, the result is a decline in total demand for goods and services, i.e., a depression. And if capitalists continue to want to save more than entrepreneurs want to invest, the depression turns into lasting stagnation such as characterized the 1930s.

Keynes, of course, had a lot to say about the behavior and motivations of entrepreneurs and capitalists, some of it insightful and even brilliant, but much also banal and in the style of traditional neoclassical theory. From a Marxist point of view a crucial weakness of Keynes was that, like all bourgeois thought, he was unable to treat these problems *historically*. He understood the depression decade remarkably well, but he did not understand how and where it fitted into the overall history of capitalism. This is at least one reason why the relevance of Keynes has often seemed rather narrowly limited to that troubled period.

---

*Neoclassical theory, as we have seen, assigned this function to the rate of interest. Keynes's reasons for rejecting this solution were complicated and cannot be dealt with here. But apart from—and in addition to—Keynes there is a compelling reason for denying to the rate of interest a role in equilibrating saving and investment. Orthodox theory holds that less will be saved the lower the rate of interest and vice versa. But this ignores the fact that under capitalism most saving is motivated not by considerations of consumption (now or in the future) but by a drive to accumulate wealth as a source of social standing, power, security, etc. This being the case, a lower rate of interest is likely to be a signal to save more, not less, out of current income.

The Great Depression was ended, not by a spontaneous resurgence of the accumulation process but by the Second World War. And for reasons often analyzed in these pages, the war itself brought about vast changes in almost every aspect of the world capitalist system. Much capital was destroyed; the diversion of production to wartime needs left a huge backlog of unfilled consumer demand; both producers and consumers were able to pay off debts and build up unprecedented reserves of cash and borrowing power; important new industries (e.g., jet planes) grew from military technologies; drastically changed power relations between and among victorious and defeated nations gave rise to new patterns of trade and capital flows. In a real sense, world capitalism was reborn on new foundations and entered a period in important respects similar to that of its early childhood.

In particular the relationship between the demand for and supply of investment capital, which had been so unfavorable to the performance of the system during most of the interwar period, was suddenly reversed. Once again, demand seemed practically unlimited, supply painfully restricted. A secular investment boom developed, to a significant extent self-reinforcing and further fueled by major wars in Korea and Vietnam. For the next two decades capitalism relived its golden age.

Bourgeois economists, not surprisingly, heaved a figurative sigh of relief and quietly fell back into their accustomed ways of thinking. Neoclassical economics staged a comeback; Keynesians, with few exceptions, backed off from what they had earlier hailed as the "Keynesian revolution," regarding it as the reaction to a set of highly exceptional and strictly temporary conditions. The heretical ideas Keynes had put forward in the 1930s for restoring a sustainable balance between saving and investment—redistribution of income to increase consumption and curtail saving, government participation in and controls over investment—were quickly forgotten. Increasing inequality of income and wealth was restored to good standing as a worthy goal and in due course became official government policy under the likes of Margaret Thatcher and Ronald Reagan.

So, where do we stand now? Here are a few conclusions that emerge from applying the foregoing theoretical/historical analysis to the actual performance of capitalism during the past decade.

(1) Capitalism's post-Second World War boom came to an end in the early 1970s and was followed by a resumption of the stagnation which had been interrupted by the war. The cause of this stagnation was the same as before, a persistent and growing imbalance between the demand for and supply of investment capital. This imbalance is rooted in the fundamental tendencies of maturing capitalism that were analyzed above.

(2) On the demand side, the need for new investment, relative to the size of the system as a whole, has steadily declined and has now reached an historic low. The reproduction of the system is largely self-financing (through depreciation reserves), and existing industries are for the most part operating at low levels of capacity utilization. New industries, on the other hand, are not of the heavy capital-using type and generate a relatively minor demand for additional capital investment.

(3) On the supply side, the size of the pool of liquid capital available for new investment has never been as great as it is today. There are two sets of facts that clearly point to this conclusion and at the same time reflect the causal factors at work: (a) The process of concentration and centralization of wealth and income has continued and reached new heights in the post-Second World War period. The main facts in this respect were summarized in an article by Jerry Kloby, "The Growing Divide: Class Polarization in the 1980s" (MR, September 1987). An inevitable consequence is the swelling of the pool of fresh savings seeking profitable investment outlets. However, since the demands on this pool for investment in the production of real goods and services have been declining, more and more of it has been flowing into purely financial

channels, giving rise to a vast expansion of the financial superstructure of the economy and an unparalleled explosion of speculative activity of all kinds.

(b) With demand declining and supply increasing, the real process of capital accumulation has sunk into a rut of stagnation the depth of which is only partly obscured by an unprecedented peacetime military buildup heavily dependent on government deficit financing.

This, then, is where we stand today. Apart from the financial explosion which—for reasons that cannot be explored here—was absent in the Great Depression, the situation is basically similar to that which existed in the late 1930s. The "solution" then was world war. Given capitalism's long and blood-soaked history, it would be natural to assume that this will happen again. But by what may well be history's greatest irony, the atom bomb that signalled the end of the Second World War has thrown up an apparently insuperable barrier to a repetition of that earlier experience. Not that an attempt at repetition is impossible, but what *is* unlikely is that it would be a solution for capitalism (or anything else). This is not to argue the obsolescence of war as such, only that it is increasingly obvious, even to the U.S. ruling class, that war on a scale adequate to provide capitalism with an escape from its present impasse is no longer a rational option.

What is the alternative?

Keynes pointed the way 50 years ago—redistribution of income and public control over the investment process. That under appropriate conditions this approach can work is not open to doubt. Not of course because it was adopted at the time Keynes suggested it—far from it. Even Roosevelt's New Deal shunned such "radical" policies. But it was precisely this approach that was forced by circumstances on those who became responsible for managing the economy in the Second World War. Enormous increases in government revenues were required, and this necessitated fiscal and monetary policies that diverted purchasing power from all classes, but especially the wealthy, into the hands of the government. And to make sure that the spending of these funds would call forth the desired mix of output of war goods and the means to produce them, far-reaching controls had to be imposed on all key sectors of the economy.

The results of these policies were immediate and dramatic. In the United States, for example, Gross National Product (measured in 1982 dollars) jumped from $717 billion in 1939, the last prewar year, to $1,381 billion in 1944, an increase of 93 percent in only five years. During the same period, unemployment plunged from 17.2 percent of the labor force to 1.2 percent, about as low as it can go.

After the war, of course, all these wartime policies were abandoned, and in this respect the situation reverted more or less rapidly to the status quo ante. As far as the general state of the economy is concerned, however, the relapse into stagnation was delayed by the postwar boom which we have already discussed. It was not until the 1970s and 1980s that we can speak of a full return to capitalist normality.

What lessons can we learn from this half century of experience that began in the 1930s and came full circle in the 1980s?

First and foremost, of course, that a fully matured capitalist economy such as we have in this country, if left to follow its own inner logic, will remain bogged down in deepening stagnation. This, in our view, is the essential starting point of any serious discussion of the present economic situation and the prospects for the period ahead.

Second, it takes a very powerful "external" force, like the Second World War or the many-sided shakeup of the global economy that followed it, to shunt the economy onto a different path. Even large regional wars like Korea and Vietnam would not be sufficient by themselves.

Third, a new world war, while not impossible, would destroy civilization as we know it in today's conditions. In an analysis of this kind, we not only can but must abstract from the possibility.

Fourth, no modern society is likely to tolerate deepening stagnation forever. Sooner or later countermeasures of one sort or another are bound to be tried. In the United States this already began to happen with the election of Reagan, with the action taking the form of a huge peacetime military buildup paid for by "Keynesian" deficit financing. It has had some very partial and temporary success (compared to Western Europe which, so far, has done practically nothing, and where unemployment has been rising for eight years in a row and now stands at approximately 11 percent), but at the cost of side effects—like an unprecedented debt explosion—that are threatening to derail the whole strategy. One faction of the U.S. ruling class seems to favor fleeing forward into such desperate adventures as the Strategic Defense Initiative, known also as Star Wars. Other factions, while recognizing the insanity of this course, have no alternatives to propose and show no signs of attempting to develop one.

In these circumstances, it seems to us that it is incumbent on the Left to come up with proposals that (1) address the real problem, (2) recognize that it stems from the very nature of the system and hence cannot be "solved" by superficial reforms, and yet (3) work to defend the interests of the victims of the system's failure while preparing them for the revolutionary changes that in the long run will be essential.

This is the challenge facing the Left. At a time when the rulers of the country are floundering around in a state bordering on complete intellectual and political bankruptcy, meeting the challenge in a straightforward and *radical* way—there really is no other way—will not bring us any kudos or rewards from the powers that be, but it could give us a renewed sense of purpose that has been so painfully lacking in a period that future historians may well come to call the decline and fall of the American empire.

(September 7, 1987)

The Stock Market Crash and Its Aftermath

Panic is but a step away from euphoria in a market that has run amok. History has demonstrated time and again that manic speculation produces violent reactions. In this respect, the recent stock market collapse is no exception. Why it happened precisely when it did is of little relevance, since sooner or later the turn from euphoria to panic was inevitable. What happened this time, however, was not just another pricking of a speculative bubble. In the present global context, the stock market crash in the citadel of capitalism threatened to disrupt the whole world's financial system.

The main danger stemmed from the close ties that exist between the stock market and the banks. Security dealers need to borrow heavily for their day-to-day operations, and the gamblers play in the Wall Street casino with money supplied by the banks. When share prices plunged on October 19, 1987, with no bottom in sight, the assets pledged to the banks by stock market operators as collateral for their loans vanished in a matter of hours. As it happens, the leading banks had been skating on thin ice for a long time because of the inability of third world and some large domestic borrowers to service their debts, and the banks' reliance in their turn on short-term borrowed money.* In the midst of these constraints the actual and potential drain of huge loan losses arising from the stock-market crash brought the banks closer to the brink. Meanwhile, not only were the major market operators unable to

*See "Banks: Skating on Thin Ice," in this space, MR, February 1975; reprinted in our book, *The End of Prosperity* (MR Press, 1977).

repay their debts, they needed still more loans to stay afloat, let alone to try to stem the downward spiral. But the bankers were unable or unwilling to grant further loans to a panic-stricken market. In short, the market break on October 19 set off a chain reaction that became even more ominous on the following day. What prevented this chain reaction from developing into a full-scale meltdown* was the prompt intervention of the Federal Reserve, which poured many billions of dollars into the system. It was this fresh infusion of new money into the banks and security firms that kept the financial crisis from going completely out of control.

The rescue operation was preceded by an unprecedented, one-sentence statement by Alan Greenspan, the recently installed chairman of the Federal Reserve Board, issued in the morning of the second day of the crisis. It said: "The Federal Reserve, consistent with its responsibilities as the nation's central bank, affirmed today its readiness as a source of liquidity to support the economic and financial system." Greenspan's choice of words is especially noteworthy. Normally, government officials and business leaders try to allay panic with calming statements. In the case of a severe break in the stock market, one might expect declarations minimizing its significance and potential impact. But here was the head of the central bank implying that the stability of the whole *economic and financial system* was at stake. Although Greenspan did not spell out whether he was referring only to the United States, he undoubtedly had in mind the menace to the world capitalist economy, especially in view of the speed with which the panic spread to the stock markets and banking communities of other centers of capital—to Japan, England, Germany, France, Switzerland, the Netherlands, etc.

The Fed's implicit admission of the extent of the crisis was echoed with even greater emphasis and in a more forthright

---

*The word "meltdown" was coined to describe what would happen if a nuclear chain reaction in a power plant went out of control. After October 19 it came increasingly into use as a metaphor for an uncontrollable interconnected chain of events that would result in a closing down of the financial system. Thus, John Phelan, Jr., chairman of the New York Stock Exchange, declared at the end of trading on Black Monday: "It's the nearest thing to a meltdown that I want to see."

way by the Task Force on Market Mechanisms set up by President Reagan on the heels of the disaster to analyze what had happened. The five members of the task force—heads of major investment firms and giant manufacturing corporations—are hardly scaremonger types, yet the conclusions they reached were indeed alarming. As summarized in the *Wall Street Journal* (January 11, 1988), their report of findings noted:

> Monday, October 19 was perhaps the worst day in the history of U.S. equity markets. . . . By midday Tuesday the financial system was on the brink of collapse. . . . But even more serious . . . was the fact that the crisis was on the brink of imperiling the world financial system. . . . Because of the near shutdown of the markets, a widespread credit breakdown seemed likely. . . . The financial system was close to gridlock.

But the fact that a total meltdown was prevented and that stock prices, though highly volatile, have recovered from the October 20 low do not signify that the market crisis is over. In this connection it is worth recalling the 1929 experience. The day of reckoning then fell on October 29, which until the recent events was seen as "the most devastating day in the history of the New York stock market" (John Kenneth Galbraith, *The Great Crash*, p. 116). The panic, however, lasted only a few days. And in less than two weeks share prices stopped falling, to be followed by a strong recovery. It soon seemed that the sick market was restored to health and that things were back to normal. The apparent normalcy, however, lasted only five months, during which share prices rose almost 50 percent (as measured by the Dow-Jones average, from November 13, 1929, to April 17, 1930). The recovery turned out to be only an interlude before the full meaning of the original crash revealed itself. Starting in the spring of 1930, the market sank slowly and inexorably for two full years. In the summer of 1932 the average share price was 86 percent below the 1929 high. The Dow-Jones average of industrial stock prices did not get back to its 1929 level until 1954.

A similar pattern of protracted decline was the outstanding feature of the Great Depression as a whole. At first, the decline in production and employment in 1930 had the appearance of an orderly business cycle recession. There were even signs in the spring of that year that recovery might be in sight. But this was a mirage: the 17 percent reduction of manufacturing production in 1930 was followed by a 21 percent drop in 1931. The contraction continued until 1932, by which time manufacturing production was only half that of 1929. And even though production began to turn upward after 1932, the index of manufacturing activity did not reattain its previous peak until eight years later.

In recounting this history we do not mean to imply that it is necessarily a scenario of what lies ahead. Rather, it is to suggest two realistic possibilities: first, that all the consequences of the October events may not be seen for some time to come; and second, that dramatic breaks are not necessarily the most important aspects of an unraveling crisis. Much more significant is the slow and protracted deterioration of financial and economic affairs.

At the present time, speculation is still rampant throughout the capitalist world, and plain sailing for the capitalist financial system is by no means assured. Indeed, the main message of the report of the President's Task Force is that the October crash may recur. A major reason, as the authors of the report explain, is that the financial innovations of the last ten years, ostensibly designed to help maintain orderly markets, turned out to be major contributors to disorder. Without dwelling on the details of these innovations (such as futures linked to indexes of stock prices), the important thing to understand is that gambling in these instruments requires cash advances of as little as 5 to 10 percent of the price of the contract, the rest being borrowed from banks or security firms. Working with such slim margins, skillful traders can amass huge profits as long as prices continue to move up. But by the same token, their losses can be enormous when the market turns sour. Traders in futures and other instruments based on borrowing to the hilt are then trapped: as the value of the collateral underlying their debt evaporates, they are compelled to dump their contracts or face losing all the cash they advanced as well as what they borrowed. Selling pressure from this source helped to create the October panic, as is fully substantiated in the Task Force report. Nonetheless, it didn't take long after the shakeup for the gambling casino to resume operating in much the same way as it had earlier. And for this reason, among others, the possibility of another major market break cannot be dismissed.

Another possible trigger of further financial disorder can come from developments abroad. Just as Black Monday sent aftershocks around the world, a major upset in a foreign market can take its toll here. This is especially true of the impact that can come from such a major player in international finance as Japan. In this connection, an article in *The Economist* (November 17, 1987) entitled "A Crash Waiting to Happen" merits close attention. The subject is the way the Tokyo stock market returned to manic speculation soon after the October events:

> This week Japan's triumphant collective optimists paid $38 billion for another privatized 12-1/2 percent tranche of the state's telephone company, Nippon Telegraph and Telephone. . . . Each NTT share [was sold] for $19,000—the equivalent of *270 years'-worth of the profits currently accruing to that share.* . . . Today . . . Japanese investors seem starry-eyed even by their own cosmic standards. For much of the past decade the average price-earnings ratio on the Nikkei index [of stock prices in Japan] has swung between 20 and 30; this year's range is between 55 and 70. The ratio of share price to underlying net assets were usually around two. Now, even post-crash, it is 3-1/2. *(Emphasis added.)*

Nor are domestic and foreign stock markets the only places where mania can turn into panic. The government securities and foreign-exchange markets, awash with debt-based instruments (futures, options, and futures on options), are hotbeds of speculation. Giant corporations as well as commercial and investment banks are playing with fire in the $200 billion-a-day foreign-exchange market. Nor should one ignore the inflation of real estate prices here and abroad. The latest madness in this area is particularly obvious in the dizzy heights reached in Japan: good land in Tokyo now sells for over $216,000 a *square yard.* By no means does this exhaust the list of potential disaster locations. The point is that the global financial system now appears to be more fragile than ever in view of the high degree of internationalization of capital markets and the extent to which financial institutions are involved directly and indirectly in hectic speculative activities. This being the case, it may yet turn out that the October crash was not the last act, but merely the prelude.

Why has the financial world arrived at such an impasse? Is it an aberration—a conjuncture of accidental factors that will subside with the passage of time, as most mainstream economists seem to assume? Or is it perhaps the result of deepseated causes that have long been and continue to be in operation?

As a preliminary to answering this question, it needs to be emphasized that risk and uncertainty permeate all the pores of a market economy. Almost every decision about capital investment, production schedules, inventory policy, prices, and distribution requires taking chances that will affect the extent of profit or loss. This risk-taking environment is made to order for widespread speculation throughout the economic system—in stocks, bonds, real estate, commodities, foreign exchange, etc. There are two sides to this rampant speculation. On the one hand, it helps to keep the economic wheels moving; on the other, it generates instability. By its very nature, speculation leads to excesses that accelerate and overextend the expansion phase of business cycles and conversely exaggerate the depth and length of the downswing.

So much for what is normal in capitalism. What has happened in the last few years, however, is quite different. The degree and extent of speculation have far exceeded what could be considered normal. Yet when placed in historical perspective, this seeming abnormality can be seen to be a direct and logical product of a new stage of economic development which began when the world economy began to run out of steam after twenty-five years of rapid growth following the end of the Second World War. The powerful forces that had supported this long wave of prosperity petered out, and no new stimuli appeared to generate capital investment sufficient to sustain a continuation of vigorous growth. The options for capitalist societies in such circumstances are few. A profit-directed economy, driven by the imperative to accumulate capital and the pressures of competition, cannot stand still. It either expands or slumps. In practice, the downward slide began in the early 1970s. All the leading capitalist nations entered a long period of shrinking growth rates, accompanied by rising mass unemployment and oppressive global overcapacity. What prevented this creeping stagnation from turning into a full-scale depression was a debt explosion and a dizzying spiral of speculation. Inevitably, this "solution" in turn became the problem.

Assumption of an ever increasing debt load became the way of life in every sphere of the economy: government, industry, agriculture, personal consumption, and even finance. Debt is of course not necessarily dangerous. In fact, it is necessary and useful when the forces underlying capital accumulation are strong and well-founded. Debt is then part of a process that produces substantial growth in income, thereby providing the means for repayment. But neither is debt in and of itself any kind of a cure-all. In a weak economy, saddled with excess capacity and lacking important new channels of capital investment, the stimulus supplied by debt soon wears out. In this situation, the economy tends to become addicted to debt: more and more is needed just to keep the engine going.

The evidence of such addiction in the present stage of stagnation is clear enough. Since the early 1970s, and much more so in the 1980s, the pace of debt accumulation has accelerated to the point where it far exceeds the sluggish expansion of the underlying "real" economy. Financial troubles were bound to develop in an economy so dependent on debt. The most dramatic symptoms of these strains showed up in failures and near bankruptcies of both borrowers and lenders, for example: Penn Central (1970), Lockheed (1971), Franklin National Bank (1974), Chrysler (1979), First Pennsylvania Bank (1980), Penn Square Bank (1982), and the Continental Illinois Corporation (1984). In the midst of general instability, the failure of a sizable company can have a far-reaching impact, setting off a chain reaction that can bring down key economic spheres. Impending dangers of this sort, however, have been headed off by government rescue operations of the more important large firms that were on the brink of going under.

Although these emergency measures plugged holes in the dike, something more was needed to sustain the flood of debt, a function performed by inflation—a spiralling of prices of commodities and assets. As far as commodity prices are concerned, the tie-in is simple. Higher prices raise the level of national income and reduce the value of the dollar. Borrowers are thus able to service their old debts with cheaper dollars. The major assistance from this source came in the 1970s. Between 1970 and 1980 consumer prices more than doubled, advancing 112 percent. The rate of increase slowed down after that: prices rose only 40 percent between 1980 and 1987. In view of this retardation, the inflation of assets became an ever more important consequence of the debt explosion. Consumers could borrow more by obtaining second mortgages based on the higher market value of their homes. Similarly, business firms and speculators were able to obtain more credit because they were able to back it with higher priced collateral.

What evolved was a closely interconnected set of financial relations. Price inflation spurred speculation in natural resources, real estate, stocks, and other assets. In turn, the resulting rise in asset values fanned the flames of speculation. And both inflation and speculation contributed to the growth of borrowing, while providing the needed framework for a continuing debt explosion.

Growth in the demand for credit was only one side of the financial coin. On the other side was a ballooning of supply of financial instruments as competition heated up to make the most of the profit opportunities. Competition grew between commercial banks, investment banks, finance companies, and the financial systems of different nations. Nor was this all. Nonfinancial firms, faced with stagnation in their traditional spheres of activity, got into the act as well. Industrial corporations used their cash reserves to buy banks, finance companies, real estate and insurance firms, and stock market operators. But the severity of competition tended to reduce profit margins in conventional money-market activity. As a result, aggressive innovation in the financial sphere came more and more to the forefront. Starting in the 1970s, the financial markets have been inundated with new instruments to stimulate speculation. Moreover, the floodgates of competition and speculation have been widened as restrictive regulations, instituted in the hope of avoiding the financial disasters of the Great Depression, were eliminated or eased in one national center of capital after another.

What is essentially new in the present economic situation is that the center and focus of the capitalist economy has shifted from the production of goods and services to the buying, selling, and multiplication of financial assets. The traditional imperative to accumulate capital geared to providing plants and equipment that yield a future stream of income and jobs has been replaced by the drive to accumulate money capital *per se*— in a world far removed from productive activity. Real wealth in capitalism grows from an expansion of the mass of surplus value created in the process of production. But in today's world ruled by finance, the underlying growth of surplus value falls increasingly short of the rate of accumulation of money capital. In the absence of a base in surplus value, the money capital amassed becomes more and more nominal, indeed fictitious. It comes from the sale and purchase of paper assets, and is based on the assumption that asset values will be continuously inflated. What we have, in other words, is ongoing speculation grounded in the belief that, despite fluctuations in price, asset values will forever go only one way—upward! Against this background, the October stock market crash assumes a far-reaching significance. By demonstrating the fallacy of an unending upward movement in asset values, it exposes the irrational kernel of today's economy.

Although the real meaning of the stock market crash is not yet generally recognized, there is a heightened awareness of the critical problems facing today's economy. It is true that the media have been emphasizing for a long time the difficulties created by government and trade deficits, instability of the foreign-exchange value of the dollar, high interest rates, etc. But these troubles seemed less ominous when viewed against the background of the euphoria on the stock markets around the world: buoyant markets encouraged the belief that before long the economy as a whole would pick up steam and current ills would somehow be cured along the way. The crash not only cast doubt on such wishful thinking, but also caused more and more observers to begin wondering whether there is any feasible way out of the plight into which the economy has fallen.

There are sound reasons for such worries since each proposed remedy is full of contradictions.

The massive federal government deficit is a case in point. As we have pointed out on more than one occasion in this space, the government deficit is far from being a primary trouble spot. In fact it serves as an important counteracting force to the prevailing stagnation. On the other hand, the business community here and abroad sees the deficit, presumably because of its effect on interest rates, as a crucial cause of instability in the capitalist world as a whole. No doubt this perception, regardless of its accuracy, influences business decisions. Nevertheless, the elimination or sizable reduction of the deficit would remove a key prop to demand, and is therefore notably dangerous at a time when an economic recession is already overdue. What we said in an earlier discussion of the deficit still holds: "Today's capitalism . . . can't live without the deficits and it can't live with them" ("The Federal Deficit: The Real Issues," MR, April 1984).

The trade deficit poses an equally if not more formidable dilemma. Given the extraordinarily complicated nature of the problem, it is even questionable whether anything short of a severe recession could seriously reduce the present huge excesses of imports over exports. Not so long ago this deficit was supposed to be due to the lack of competitiveness of U.S. industry, stemming from too high wages and too low productivity. But this simplistic view has been appearing less frequently in the last year or so. It is now generally recognized that the earlier rise in the international value of the dollar was an important cause of the trade gap. But for three years now the exchange value of the dollar has been falling and the trade deficit remains as sticky as ever. In fact it has grown substantially in these three years. But let us assume for the sake of argument that the trade gap can eventually be eliminated or reduced to a negligible amount. For that to happen the rest of the world would have to digest an enormous volume of imports from the United States while at the same time reducing their exports to this country. That would deal a crippling blow to the ability of debt-laden third world countries to service their debts and at the same time add greatly to the troubles of U.S. banks. Nor would the advanced capitalist countries be any more pleased by such a solution of the U.S. trade deficit. They too are in the midst of stagnation, mass unemployment, and excess productive capacity. A reversal of their trade trends, i.e., a cut in exports and a rise in imports, could easily bring on a severe depression in view of the extent to which their economies depend on an export surplus. A harmonious resolution of the conflicting interests on trade between the United States and the other major powers is clearly not in the cards. On the contrary, any significant reduction in the U.S. trade deficit would more probably be the prelude to an outburst of trade wars.

As it is, the tensions between the United States and its major trading partners are all too numerous. A healthy proportion of the dollars earned by the trade-surplus countries are returned to this country to purchase treasury securities, stocks, real estate, and manufacturing enterprises. In the absence of this flow of capital to the United States, the international value of the dollar would go into a tailspin, in the course of which international trade and finance would be severely disrupted. Meanwhile, Washington flails about trying to get its allies to alter their trade and interest policies in order to alleviate U.S. difficulties. On the other hand, the other nations insist that the United States straighten out its own affairs, thus hopefully restimulating the world economy. Since both sides suffer from illusions about the practical possibility of making progress along the lines they propose, the tensions that threaten ultimately to break out in trade and currency wars keep mounting.

The point is that none of the predicaments facing the United States is solvable in a stagnating world economy. It appears that the two deficits are both essential, the one to keep the economy of the United States from collapsing, the other to keep the rest of the world from collapsing.

In this situation, the attention of economists, politicians, and media experts in the United States has been turning to the search for a way to restructure the U.S. economy in a radically new direction. A typical example is the lead story in *Business Week* of November 16, 1987, less than a month after the crash. The headline reads as follows: "*It's time for America to wake up. The message is clear: Americans have spent too much, borrowed too much, and imported too much. Now it has to stop.*" Although the hard edges of the proposed remedies are sometimes smoothed over, the main thrust is clear: consumption has to be reduced. And to this end wages have to be held down and government spending on subsidies, welfare, and social security programs lowered.

The supposed rationale for this approach is that less consumption will result in more savings and hence increased investment, leading to a resurgence of growth. Economic growth in the United States will pull the whole world with it, and all the problems of a stagnant global economy will gradually evaporate.

The trouble with this reasoning of course is that higher savings do not bring about more investment. The causal relation is rather the other way around: when investment increases, incomes (especially corporate profits) increase and so do savings. What propels investment is not savings but attractive profit opportunities. And by the same token, what has been holding back investment in the period of stagnation is the lack of opportunities for profitable productive activity. Proposed remedies aimed at reducing consumption would merely further reduce the stimulus to invest.

Some of the more perceptive observers of the economic scene are aware of this paradox, and are counting on a big jump in exports to stimulate higher investment. But as already noted above, exports large enough to perform this function would create havoc in the rest of the world, with the result of a severe contraction in the markets for our exports.

The simple fact is that there is no growth miracle available. The notion that the world economy can be shifted into high gear under present circumstances is pure illusion. And if anything is crystal clear, it is that belt-tightening surely offers no way out.

If the stock market crash teaches anything, it is that the mess the economy is in flows not from excessive consumption but from capitalism's ruthless pursuit of unlimited wealth by any and all available means, whether or not these have anything to do with satisfying the needs of real human beings. The only remedy for *this* situation is a truly revolutionary reconstruction of the whole socio-economic system.

History shows that such fundamental transformations take a long time to accomplish. It is reason, however, not history that tells us that the time will be shorter the more clearly the victims of the outworn system see the need for the change. In the meantime, they have a dual task: to learn about the need for a new system and to struggle to protect themselves against the ravages of the old.

(February 1, 1988)

The Great Malaise

The above title is taken from a short article published just eight years ago (March-April 1980) in *Challenge* magazine.* What is amazing about the article is its uncanny prescience; what is ironical is that as Chairman of the Fed, hence the world's top central banker, Mr. Greenspan is playing out the role he foresaw the central bankers of the world would be forced into—with consequences far removed from anything he, or anyone else for that matter, could consider desirable.

In the spring of 1980, half a year before Reagan was first elected President, the U.S. economy was going into its sharpest recession since the Second World War. The business world was deeply worried: could this be the start of a replay of the Great Depression of a half a century earlier? This was the question with which Alan Greenspan was concerned. Here is how he introduced it:

October 29, 1979 marked [the anniversary of] the beginning of the greatest economic upheaval of modern history. The contractions and financial panics that took place in the United States prior to the Great Depression were contemporaneously perceived as deep and prolonged, as indeed they were. All fell far short, however, the devastation that took hold beginning with the collapse of stock prices fifty years ago. Today's conventional view is that the legislative response to that trauma—deposit insurance to prevent runs on banks, securities legislation to stem stock market speculation, and sophisticated monetary tools to prevent credit panics—will prevent such a disaster from confronting us again. In any event, let us not

*Since this article was written, *Challenge* has reprinted "The Great Malaise" in its 30th anniversary issue (March-April 1988).

forget that the crash of 1929 and the despair that followed was, in itself, a rare event, one which would have been unlikely to be replicated, even with the institutional structure that prevailed in the 1920s and earlier. The danger currently confronting us, in my judgment, is not a deflation of the 1930s type; rather it is the consequence of excessively inflationary policies which are being rushed into place in response to a credit crisis which is perceived as a replay of the Great Depression.

Greenspan next went on to note that stock-market specu-
lation leading up to the collapse of October 1929, which nearly everyone agreed was crucial in bringing on the Depression, was not a factor in 1980: "Unlike the period of mid-1929, equity prices relative to earnings are now low, great caution prevails, and few, if any, observers would ascribe speculative excesses to the current stock market."

But there were excesses elsewhere which threatened the stability of the U.S. economy, and here Greenspan selected five developments for special consideration. These were (1) real estate speculation, (2) the related ballooning of mortgage and consumer debt in relation to household incomes, (3) the sinking deeper and deeper into debt of non-oil-producing third-world countries (today's more general third-world debt crisis was still two years in the future), (4) the increasing vulnerability of the complex and little-understood Eurocurrency system, and (5) the so-called dollar-overhang problem—in Greenspan's words, "the evident excess of dollar-denominated assets in government and private portfolios throughout the world."

As Greenspan saw it, some combination of these growing imbalances could—at times he even seemed to imply that it necessarily would—trigger a "cascading set of bankruptcies," precisely the process that ushered in the massive credit defla-
tion that turned into the Great Depression. But Greenspan didn't think it would be allowed to work out this way. At one point he spoke of "the major central bankers, of course, hav[ing] contingency plans which would be immediately implemented in the event of a cascading series of financial failures in the Eurocurrency markets." At another point, near the end of the

article, he spelled this out more specifically, drawing the conclusion that provided the article with its title:

> With the world's central bankers standing ready to flood the world's economies with paper claims at the first sign of a problem, a full-fledged credit deflation reminiscent of the 1930s seems out of the question. . . . The overriding mandate of the world's monetary authorities to prevent a credit deflation almost assures policy overkill at the first sign of credit stringency and falling prices. Deflation would be quickly aborted—to be followed shortly by accelerating inflation and economic stagnation. In despair, policy-makers, I fear, are likely to retreat to increased symptom-fighting—price, wage, and credit controls—and a broad expansion of economic regimentation. Such a response would reinforce the stagnation and economic malaise.

> Thus in today's political and institutional environment, a replay of the Great Depression is the Great Malaise. It would not be a period of falling prices and double-digit unemployment, but rather an economy racked with inflation, excessive unemployment (8 to 9 percent), falling productivity, and little hope for a more benevolent future.

Having led his readers up to this dismal conclusion, Greenspan at the very last minute relented. Here is his final paragraph, evidently intended as an antidote to the preceding pages of bad news and gathering doom:

> I should like to emphasize that a breakdown of the world financial and economic systems is still a low-probability outcome. There is a remarkable resiliency in the basic capitalist institutions which support most Western societies. Extraordinary shocks are required to undermine them. While I do not want to appear the protagonist for Pollyanna, I trust that in a hundred years Black Friday will *still* be regarded as the beginning of the greatest economic upheaval in modern history.

It is now eight years later. How has Alan Greenspan's analysis stood the test of time? The answer to this question would be interesting in any case, but it surely gains in interest from the fact that Greenspan is now the world's most powerful central banker.

To begin with, we need to note some salient facts from the history of these eight years. First, and far from least important, all the troublesome trends the author focused on in 1980 have continued to operate: real estate speculation, the growth of mortgage and consumer debt in relation to household in-comes the sinking of the third world deeper into debt, the growing vulnerability of the Eurocurrency system, and the piling up of dollars and dollar-denominated assets in govern-ment and private portfolios around the world. All of these problem areas are still with us, all more threatening than ever. But there are others, invisible or just beginning to loom up on the horizon in 1980, that have grown to enormous proportions in the ensuing years: (1) the spread of speculation from real estate to stocks and a bewildering assortment of relatively new financial instruments such as options, futures, and swaps; (2) the burgeoning federal deficit with its resultant more-than-doubling of the national debt; and (3) the unprecedented trade deficit which in an astonishingly short time has transformed the United States from the world's largest creditor into its largest debtor.

All of these developments, while of course absent from Greenspan's analysis, have powerfully reinforced the main thrust of his argument—so much so in fact that taken together with the forces already at work in 1980, they have driven the top-heavy financial superstructure of the American economy into precisely the denouement which Greenspan in 1980 still regarded as a "low-probability outcome."

The break when it came took place in the same place as in 1929, the stock market. As we have argued at some length, the "meltdown" which almost took place on the New York Stock Exchange on October 19, 1987, would have been the beginning of the "cascading set of bankruptcies" Greenspan had warned of in his article. And the monetary authorities, this time represented by Greenspan himself, were every bit as alert and ready to intervene as Greenspan had assumed they would be eight years earlier. We remind you again of the statement he issued on that fateful day: "The Federal Reserve, consistent with its responsibilities as the nation's central bank, affirmed today its readiness as a source of liquidity to support the economic and financial system." This prompt and decisive action accomplished what it was intended to: the cascade was blocked before it started, the deflation was aborted before it was conceived.

What about Greenspan's concept of the Great Malaise which was intended to tell us what comes after the deflation abortion? Here, in our opinion, Greenspan's vision is seriously flawed in at least one important respect. At several places in the article, including those quoted above, he expresses a strong belief that one of the main consequences of aborting deflation was bound to be inflation, beginning early and becoming a chronic feature of the Great Malaise to follow. This belief is presumably the product of the conventional monetarist theory that inflation automatically results from increases in the money supply. If this were true, Greenspan would surely be right since aborting deflation involves, as he puts it in one of the passages quoted above, "standing ready to flood the world's economies with paper claims"—i.e., with credit money—which is exactly what he announced as Fed policy on October 19th and actually carried out to the tune of many billions of dollars.

But monetarist theory is simply wrong. The relation between the money supply (however defined) and inflation is very variable depending on conditions existing at any given time: it can be what monetarist theory assumes it has to be, but it can also be quite different. And in the conditions of a credit crisis, it certainly won't conform to the theory. In fact, in an atmosphere of fear and uncertainty such as characterizes a credit crisis, it is hard to imagine what could ignite inflation, i.e., let loose a surge of demand for all kinds of commodities and assets. It might conceivably be accomplished by a deliberate policy of inundating the economy with paper money, but this would involve a total subversion of all the rules and regulations governing the present monetary system, and it would be anathema to the conservative central bankers and finance ministers (men like Greenspan himself) who are in charge of this system. If anything is clear, it is that in the kind of financial crisis contemplated in Greenspan's article and actually realized in the aftermath of the crash of 1987, his fear of "accelerating inflation" is indeed misplaced.

The elimination of the inflation bogey, however, in no way negates the Great Malaise scenario. On the contrary, it only makes it the more plausible. Even before October 19th the economy was in shaky condition, and since the crash the imbalances have multiplied. The next recession, already overdue by historical business-cycle standards, is widely expected some time this or early next year. When it does come, not only will production and incomes fall and unemployment increase but many weaknesses, now hidden or only potential, will be uncovered. Millions of households are up to their ears in debt; hundreds of banks are on the regulators' endangered lists; even many big corporations, loaded with debt during the merger and buyout binge of the last few years, are surviving by the thinnest of margins. In all too many cases a recession will be the last straw. To be sure, the government will intervene in various ways to prevent or soften these blows. But there are limits to what it can do, and it is important to understand how narrow these limits really are.

First, there will be the normal question of what to do about the recession itself, with the standard options falling within the areas of fiscal and monetary policy. With respect to the former, combatting an economic downturn calls for more government spending and/or lower taxation, in other words, a bigger deficit. But as everyone knows, the upswing that began in 1982 has been in large measure fueled by huge deficits, and political pressure to reduce them has grown to unprecedented proportions. Moreover, the pressure will doubtless be increased by the automatic tendency of recession to expand the deficit even without any change in fiscal policy.* What this implies is that the government, in order to fatten up the expansion phase of the business cycle of the 1980s, has pretty well used up the ammunition which would normally be available to fight the recession phase. Clearly, under present condi-

---

*Growing joblessness generates more spending for unemployment compensation, welfare outlays, etc., and declining incomes result in lower tax revenues—hence rising deficits.

tions, the leeway for an expansionary fiscal policy, if it exists at all, is strictly limited.

As far as monetary policy is concerned, the conventional wisdom holds that the way to combat recession is to lower interest rates by pumping up the money supply. The reasoning is that interest makes up a large part of the cost of investment in plant and equipment and that capitalists, when faced with lower costs, will expand their investment outlays and this in turn will give the economy a boost. The appropriate response to this is that sometimes it will and sometimes it won't, depending on surrounding conditions. During the 1930s, for example, interest rates were pushed down close to the vanishing point without having any noticeable effect on the devastating investment slump that characterized the Great Depression. Given the lack of profitable investment opportunities, capitalists were obviously not to be spurred into action no matter how low interest rates might fall. If we are right that in this respect the 1980s are a lot like the 1930s, it follows that not much can be expected from monetary policy as an antidote to the next recession when it comes.

The relative impotence of fiscal and monetary policies in the economic conditions of the 1980s does not mean that the government must stand idly by and watch the coming recession run its course, any more than it had to remain on the sidelines during the stock-market crash of last October. During the last two decades there have been a whole series of threatened bankruptcies of large corporations or banks or third-world countries, any on of which could have, if left unattended, touched off a chain reaction of incalculable dimensions and consequences. In every case, the government rushed to the rescue, snuffing out burning fuses before they could ignite impending explosions. With the coming of recession, situations like this are sure to proliferate and the government is equally sure to continue in its role as active intervenor. Of course, it remains an open question how effective government intervention can be in the event of a rapid sequence of breakdowns in several domestic sectors. Also uncertain is what the government can do in case of a collapse of a key financial area outside the United States, as, for example, in international banking or the foreign exchange market.

Where all this will eventually lead no one can now predict, and no useful purpose would be served by trying to project plausible or possible scenarios. One can only guess that, at a minimum, the rescue operations will be for the most part confined to large entities and institutions, that many individuals and small businesses will be allowed to go under, and that government may find itself assuming responsibility for more economic activities than any self-respecting politician would now dare to advocate.

Meanwhile, whatever the ultimate outcome, it seems reasonably clear that the present drift of events, taken together with likely government efforts to mitigate its more destructive potentialities, fits comfortably enough into Alan Greenspan's concept of the Great Malaise.

All of which of course raises many more questions than it answers. Much has been written about the Great Depression, what caused it, its inner logic, its place in the history of capitalism. The same questions, with appropriate amendments and additions, need to be raised with respect to the Great Malaise. It is a challenge not likely to be taken up by Alan Greenspan and his fellow mainstream economists: the implications and possible ramifications are far too disturbing. All the more reason, then, for our younger colleagues on the left to step into the breach.

(March 1, 1988)

Anniversary of the Crash

The stock market crash of October 19, 1987, came very close to touching off a full-fledged financial panic, which in all probability would have marked the beginning of a serious worldwide economic slump. This was the opinion of informed analysts of the economic scene at the time, and nothing has happened since to cause us to question its accuracy. What prevented the scenario from unfolding as feared was the prompt and massive intervention of the Federal Reserve, which opened its coffers to the threatened financial community, throwing tens of billions of dollars into circulation and promising more if needed.*

All of this occurred in the course of a cyclical upswing which had already lasted nearly five years (1983–87), an extraordinarily long time by historical business-cycle standards. It was therefore natural to suppose that the shock of the crash, even though panic had been averted, would hasten the onset of an overdue recession. Now, a year later, it is clear that this did not happen. The economy as a whole—measured by such conventional indexes as GNP, unemployment, and utilization of productive capacity—has remained pretty much on the pre-crash course, and in recent months, more and more commentators have been wondering whether, as one is said to have expressed it, the crash was more than a "thunderstorm on a summer day, full of sound and fury but signifying nothing."**

---

*For details, see "The Stock Market Crash and Its Aftermath," in this space, March 1988.

**"America's Capital Markets," *The Economist*, June 11, 1988. This is a lengthy, well-researched report by *The Economist's* New York correspondent, Christopher Wood.

Some of the more sanguine among them are beginning to go much further. So impressed are they by the economy's resilience that they do not hesitate to project the present economic expansion into the indefinite future, concluding that if the government continues to pursue what they consider to be appropriate policies, the economic woes of the past will evaporate. One of the boldest and possibly most influential examples of this genre is an op-ed piece in *The New York Times* of July 22, 1988, by Martin Anderson, President Reagan's domestic policy adviser in 1981–82 and now a senior fellow at the Hoover Institute on War, Revolution, and Peace, perhaps the country's most prestigious right-wing think tank. The article, entitled "Streamlining Reaganomics for the 1990s," is accompanied by a drawing showing a line chart that starts at the bottom of the page in the early 1970s and continues upward, with only a few small dips, into the twenty-first century. The subheading reads, "Sixty-one months of straight growth—'the greatest economic expansion in history,'" and the final paragraph declares, "During the last eight years, President Reagan laid down a basic economic program that, in spite of imperfections, accomplished a great deal. What we need now is advanced Reaganomics, a more sophisticated, more elegant, perhaps more complicated economic policy that will ensure continued prosperity well into the 21st century."

Heady stuff that not even the most extreme optimist would have dared commit to print in the aftermath of last year's stock market crash. And yet even Martin Anderson, for all his confidence in a streamlined Reaganomics, cannot hide a nagging worry that haunts all the prophets of endless prosperity. Tucked away in a paragraph devoted to singing the praises of economic growth as the source of all good things, there is one short sentence that threatens to negate the author's entire best-of-all-possible-worlds message: "If the economy collapses into recession, then the economic problems we are now wrestling with will overwhelm us." Quite an admission, when you take into consideration that in some two centuries of business-cycle history, there has never been an economic expansion that didn't end in recession.

Why does Martin Anderson, or anyone else for that matter, think it will or could be different this time? If he has any thoughts on this subject, he doesn't share them with us. Still, we should resist the temptation to dismiss his whole case as no more than wishful fantasy.

History doesn't always repeat itself, and maybe this is a case in point. At any rate we shouldn't rely on history alone: we should analyze the problem as it presents itself now and try to discover if there is any reasonable case for believing that history is *not* going to repeat itself, that the nearly six years without a recession might continue into the next century, in Martin Anderson's words.

We start by asking why history up to now always has repeated itself, why periods of economic expansion invariably have given way to contractions. And here we need to hark back to certain basic characteristics of the capitalist economy.

It is of course an unplanned system. But, as Adam Smith so convincingly demonstrated, it is not an unregulated system. Entrepreneurs, acting on their own, produce for markets, and markets feed back information telling them where they have produced too much and where too little. By a series of adjustments they eliminate surpluses and shortages until a system-wide general equilibrium is reached under which all commodities are produced in quantities and sold at prices that yield equivalent rates of profit. When significant changes occur, such as shifts in demand or the introduction of new methods of production, disturbing the established equilibrium, the market feedback mechanism acts to restore it on a different level without the need for any conscious intervention from outside the system.

But there is one category of markets that do not behave in this fashion or perform an equivalent equilibrating function, namely the financial markets, where the "commodity" traded is money in its various forms, including credit, the predominant form of money in advanced capitalist countries. To a certain extent, of course, borrowing and lending take place simply to facilitate the exchange of real goods and services. But this is only a small fraction of the business of the financial markets, which for the most part are devoted to providing funds for projects expected to yield a profit over a period of time in the future. These projects can be of many different descriptions. Some take the form of "real" investment in plant and equipment, while others are themselves financial in nature, like stocks and bonds, which may be bought for the underlying assets they represent or for future sale at higher prices (speculation). In any case, neither the demand for nor the supply of investment funds is regulated by the forces that operate in the markets for the goods and services society needs for its maintenance and reproduction. And experience stretching back to the beginnings of capitalism tells us that these financial markets are inherently unstable, tending always to generate cumulative processes away from, rather than toward, a stable equilibrium.*

Given the financial instability of capital markets and their major role in the modern economy, it follows that capitalism as a whole is also an unstable system, a fact amply confirmed by the history of the last two centuries. Once again, however, this does not mean that it lacks a regulatory mechanism, only that the regulatory mechanism here is very different from the textbook supply-and-demand adjustments that function in ordinary commodity markets. Cumulative processes in financial markets are brought to an end on the upside by crises and on the downside by interludes of sluggish activity during which strains and imbalances subside and conditions favorable to a new expansion merge. The regulatory mechanism activated by the inherent instability of financial markets is thus seen to be a credit cycle which is closely related to, and in some cases practically identical with, the well-known phenomenon of the business cycle, with its phases of upswing, crisis, downswing, and depression.** The credit cycle in turn forms an integral part of the regulatory principles of capitalism, flowing from its basically unplanned character, just as do the equilibrating

---

*For a fuller explanation, see Robert Pollin, "A Theory of Financial Instability," MR, December 1983.

**There are other, so-called "real," factors involved in the business cycle. Their relation to the credit cycle has been a subject of study and often debate ever since business cycles were first recognized more than a hundred years ago.

tendencies of commodity markets, which are the central preoccupation of mainstream economics.

With this much as background, we can return to the
question posed above: Is it reasonable to believe that the
recessionless economy, now nearing the end of its sixth year,
can continue into the indefinite future?

The most important thing to keep in mind is that the
whole six-year period has been dominated by precisely the
kind of expansion typical of the credit cycle. The economy
emerged from its sharpest post-Second World War recession at
the end of 1982 and since then has expanded at a steady but (by
historical standards) moderate rate. From 1982 to 1987, GNP
increased by an average rate of 7.2 percent. Total outstanding
debt, on the other hand, grew at the much higher rate of 13.3
percent.

While there is no direct causal link between the expansion
of debt and rate of growth of GNP, it is obvious that there are
many channels through which increased borrowing feeds into
the stream of spending on goods and services and, in so doing,
supports the growth of GNP. Conversely, it is clear that a
slowing down or cessation of debt expansion, not to mention of
contraction of outstanding debt, must have an adverse effect on
GNP. Under present circumstances, therefore, when the primary force at work in the economy is not a favorable long-term
investment climate such as prevailed after the Second World
War but a ballooning of debt, it is the latter that has to be the
focus of an attempt to analyze what lies ahead. Does it make
sense to suppose that a recessionary ending to the present
economic expansion can be prevented by an indefinite continuation of the debt expansion process?

Here we must first dispose of an argument popular among
conservatives, including many mainstream economists. Debt
becomes a major issue in the capitalist economy—so the
argument runs—only if it grows more rapidly than income, as
indeed has been occurring in recent years. It follows that in
order to prevent debt problems from causing trouble down the
road, it is necessary to adopt government policies—like tax
reform to stimulate saving and investment, and deregulation of

business activity—that will presumably speed up growth and allow us, as the saying goes, to "grow out" of our debt difficulties. The trouble with this line of reasoning is that policies of this kind have been pursued during Reagan's two terms in office more vigorously than ever before at the very time when overall economic expansion has been most obviously dominated by the even more rapid expansion of debt. There have been periods in the history of capitalism when growing out of debt actually happened and on a large scale, too, but to talk about it here and now is a good example of putting the cart before the horse: in this country today, debt is the motor of growth, not a by-product of growth.

The question then is whether this motor can be expected to keep running or whether it will run out of steam, causing the economy to slide into recession, with all the dire consequences foreseen by Martin Anderson.

There is no need here to review the details of the debt expansion of recent years. Suffice it to say that it has taken place in all the major categories of debt: government debt, household (including mortage) debt, nonfinancial business debt, and financial business debt.* Expansion has continued in all four categories in 1986, 1987, and the first half of 1988. Is this likely to continue into the indefinite future?

Here it is important to keep in mind that debt has not only a quantitative but also a qualitative dimension. A million-dollar debt owed by a Rockefeller is not the same as a million-dollar debt owed by an upstart real-estate developer. The former can go on borrowing long after the latter has reached his or her limit. The same holds for a corporation whose debt-to-equity ratio is 10 percent compared to a corporation with a 90 percent debt-to-equity ratio. Nor does the quality of a particular borrower's debt remain constant over time: generally speaking, the bigger the debt grows, the more the quality declines. The theoretical limit is reached when the borrower goes bankrupt, at which time both quantity and quality are

---

*Summary statistics through 1985 were provided in the Introduction to Harry Magdoff and Paul M. Sweezy, *Stagnation and the Financial Explosion*, Monthly Review Press, 1987.

radically reevaluated. But borrowing normally slows down or ceases well before the theoretical limit is reached.

There is no doubt that these generalizations apply with full force to three of the four categories of debt listed above. (Government debt, however, is a special case which requires separate consideration.) It has often been commented on that consumer demand, which normally accounts for some two-thirds of GNP, has held up remarkably well and in fact has been an important contributing factor throughout the expansion of the 1980s. It has also been noted that there is something of a paradox here since this has occurred during a period of declining real wage rates. The explanation is partly increased consumption by the rich, who have benefitted from Reagan's policies, partly the proliferation of multiple wage-earner families, and perhaps most importantly a faster rate of growth in household debt than household income. That this deterioration of the debt-to-income ratio cannot continue forever is obvious; whether it is now approaching a limit, as some observers believe, is debatable but not provable one way or the other. But it stands to reason that as long as the household debt burden rises, more and more borrowers will be forced to retrench quite apart from any hypothetical limit. In this sense, the process can be considered self-limiting rather than indefinitely extensible.

As to nonfinancial business debt, the deterioration of quality that goes along with the increase in quantity is an almost daily subject of analysis and commentary in the business and financial media. There are many reasons, but the most prominent, and probably the most important, stems from the tidal wave of mergers, acquisitions, and leveraged buyouts (LBOs) that has swept over the economy in the Reagan period. In most of these transactions, the financial arrangements have involved a substitution of debt, typically consisting of so-called junk bonds, for equity on the balance sheets of the surviving companies. Many observers expected that the October stock market crash would put an end to this kind of speculative finance, but it has not turned out that way. While individual investors have retreated in droves from the stock market, institutions like insurance companies, investment banks, and pension funds, to name the most important, have stepped up their LBO activities in search of the huge short-run profits characteristic of this business—and in the process have pushed more and more corporations to the brink of bankruptcy.

The situation is no better with respect to financial debt. Here we need only call attention to the well-publicized plight of the country's savings and loan associations, which have already exhausted the deposit-guarantee fund (FSLIC) set up to protect their deposits and have in effect become wards of the U.S. Treasury which, according to current estimates, may have to shell out anywhere from $50 to $100 billion before the mess is cleared up. Nor are things all that much better with the commercial banks which are failing at rates not seen since the Great Depression, while rescue operations are mounted to save the biggest ones, whose failure, like the threatened failure of Continental Illinois several years ago, could precipitate a general financial collapse. No wonder *The Economist's* New York correspondent—in the report on "America's Capital Markets" cited above—speaks of "the rickety structure which passes for America's financial system." This system, he adds, "is fundamentally flawed. Worse, the quality of its credit deteriorates daily."

So much for the three nongovernmental categories of debt, the expansion of which has been helping to fuel the Reagan economic recovery. They do not look like very reliable pillars of future growth.

Government debt is something else again. The federal government's debt, by far the largest part of the total government debt, has grown from $914 billion in 1980, the first year of Reagan's presidency, to $2.58 trillion in 1988, and it is still growing at a rate of around $150 billion a year. In our economic analyses in this space, we have always considered these unprecedented peacetime federal deficits to be the main factor sustaining the economic expansion of the 1980s, the prop without which the other sustaining factors would long ago have faltered, if indeed they would ever have gotten off the ground. Whether these deficits will continue in the future, and in what amounts, is therefore a crucial question. If they should be seriously curtailed, it would almost certainly precipitate a recession. On the other hand, a substantial increase would, other things remaining equal, give an impetus to continued expansion.

In seeking an answer to this question, economic considerations such as the quality of the debt are of little relevance. The federal government can always service its debt; and given the fact that failure to live up to its commitments would be a shattering blow to the whole credit structure, it can be taken for granted that it will always do so. The problem is therefore basically political in nature.

There are pressures working both for and against deficits. The political establishment, including both Republicans and Democrats, is afraid of raising taxes; the major categories of government spending have powerful constituencies; no one wants to take action that might trigger a recession. Together, these considerations work to sustain or even expand deficit spending. On the other hand, there is a widespread belief in political and financial circles around the world that the federal deficit, in conjunction with what is commonly thought to be the closely related U.S. trade deficit, constitutes a ticking time bomb that could, and if continued long enough certainly would, explode, leaving the whole incredibly complex and swollen global financial system in ruins. This belief, which seems to be growing in importance, acts as a strong deterrent to the continuation, let alone expansion, of deficit spending.

If the outcome depended entirely on the relative strength of these contending pressures within the United States, it seems likely that those supporting deficit spending would win out. It has often been remarked that deficits are like an addictive drug: it is extremely difficult to kick the habit once acquired. But not all the players in this game are in the United States. Not only are foreign investors, central banks, and governments actively involved but more to the point, they have the means at their disposal, if they choose to use them, to force the United States into courses of action it would not adopt on its own.

Here we must keep two things in mind: (1) The United States has been running balance-of-payments deficits for many years, as a result of which the rest of the world holds enormous quantities of dollars and dollar-denominated assets. (2) A large proportion of these dollar-denominated assets are U.S. treasury securities, the purchase of which by foreigners (especially Japanese) has gone a long way toward financing the U.S. budget deficits. Under these circumstances, both the dollar exchange rate and the state of the crucially important market for U.S. government securities are at the mercy of foreign financiers and their governments. All they have to do is "lose confidence" in U.S. policies for all hell to break loose— the dollar in a free fall, the bond market in a state of collapse, with direct and indirect ripple effects too awful to contemplate. And the policy they are most likely to lose confidence in is precisely U.S. fiscal policy, that which determines the amount and direction of deficit spending.

Of course, no one wants a denouement of this kind. So both sides can be expected to act—or, more accurately, continue to act—with great caution. The present stalemate may persist for quite a while yet. But as the pressures build up, it could well turn out that the U.S. hand in this global cat-and-mouse game is weaker than that of the foreigners. Something like an ultimatum might be issued—reduce your deficits, or else—and acceded to. And that could be the beginning of the next recession.

To summarize the argument to this point: Last year's stock market crash was prevented from precipitating a panic and global slump only by prompt and massive intervention by the Federal Reserve. Rescued from this threatened disaster, the economy persisted on its pre-crash course, with a continued rapid expansion of debt, private and public, providing the driving force. With respect to the various components of private debt, quantitative increase was accompanied by qualitative decline: the process generates its own limits. With respect to government debt, the limits are external—political and international in origin—but with a comparable tendency to grow more restrictive with the passage of time.

Anyone with a sense of history has felt all along that the expansion of the 1980s, prolonged and, in many ways, unique though it has been, must inevitably end in recession. What we have tried to do is to show that this perception not only stems from a reading of history but also is fully confirmed by theory and current developments.

In a sense, of course, this may seem anything but an earthshaking discovery. After all, recessions have been happening on an average of two or three times a decade for two hundred years or more. If another one is on the way, however belatedly, why make such a fuss about it?

We believe that there are two good reasons for making a fuss, the bigger the better. One is because the political Right has, for its own reasons—largely to embellish and perpetuate the myths of the Reagan era—worked hard to create a totally false impression of the U.S. economy and its future prospects. In these circumstances, it is important to drive home the point that, like death and taxes, the next recession is as close to being inevitable as anything in human affairs can be.

But there is an even more important reason that has to do with the character of the next recession. Precisely because the present expansion has been so drawn out and unprecedented, the coming recession itself will in all probability be correspondingly prolonged and unique. In the normal course of events, the expansion would have been cut short long ago, perhaps by the failure of Continental Illinois, certainly no later than the October 1987 stock market crash. In both cases, the break was prevented by the massive intervention of the government, acting mainly through the central bank. What these actions accomplished was to negate and, for the time being, suspend the normal capitalist regulatory mechanism analyzed above. The system, in a manner of speaking, was signalling that it was ripe for a crisis and a purge of the disequilibria and imbalances that had accumulated in the preceding expansion phase of the credit cycle. But, in an ironical twist, the political establishment, professedly such ardent believers in unfettered capitalism's automatic steering mechanism, stepped in to abort the crisis and set the stage for a continuation of the very disequilibrating processes that cried out for correction.

The result was predictable. As described above, the quantity of debt continued to increase while the quality deteriorated. It is now clearly only a matter of time before a new break materializes. It could be another stock market crash—many observers of the business scene confidently expect it—but it equally could occur elsewhere—in the bond market for example, a panic on the high-flying Tokyo stock market, a rapid plunge of the dollar, a refusal of Third World debtors to go on bleeding their people for the benefit of First World capitalists, the sudden bankruptcy of a huge bank or corporation. That all of these possibilities are very real, more and more discussed and worried about in the business media, only attests to the running out of the clock on the Reagan miracle.

But, you may ask, won't the powers that be step into the breach again and abort the crisis before it gets a chance to run its course? Yes, certainly. That, by now, is standard operating procedure, and it cannot be excluded that it will succeed in the same ambiguous sense that it did after the 1987 stock market crash. If so, we will have the whole process to go through again on a more elevated and more precarious level. But sooner or later, next time or further down the road, it will not succeed. The recession will then start in earnest, and Martin Anderson's worst fears will come true.

We will then face a new situation as unprecedented as the conditions from which it will have emerged. We can only hope that the chances of making sense of it and drawing useful conclusions will improve as general projections turn increasingly into concrete realities.

(September 26, 1988)